The Executive Guide to Video Teleconferencing

The Executive Guide to Video Teleconferencing

Ronald J. Bohm, Ph.D.
Lee B. Templeton

International Standard Book Number: 0-89006-148-3
Library of Congress Catalog Card Number: 84-045201

2271847

CONTENTS

FOREWORD

We first became interested in video teleconferencing in the course of our work at First Communications Group, Inc. Using our digital network, FirstNet™, we provide wideband telecommunications network services within and among metropolitan areas to organizations with private line requirements. Since many video teleconferencing applications need to be transmitted over wideband circuits, we decided to examine this potential market. Our initial market research revealed that while very few companies and institutions had adopted it, most organizations were aware of video teleconferencing, and many were considering it.

The price of many new products and technologies passes through a cycle as the product progresses from prototype, to product release, to mass market acceptance. We have seen this phenomenon countless times (pocket calculators and liquid crystal display wristwatches provide vivid examples). Video teleconferencing is no exception. Important advances have already occurred in video compression technology and inevitably will result in broad adoption of video teleconferencing as a productivity tool.

We already have seen one "energy crises" result in jet fuel and gasoline shortages and a tripling in prices. Although the price of energy has been stable for the past few years, we would not be surprised to awaken one morning to find that history has once again repeated itself. While the relation of the cost of travel to the price of video teleconferencing may not be the only factor in the decision to adopt video, it is likely that a sudden change in this relation will accelerate the use of electronic meetings.

We found considerable literature on the subject of video teleconferencing. And yet, the existing published work focused heavily on the technology — not enough was written about the management and practical issues. While the technology is necessary for success, it is not sufficient. We saw the need for a book which would help a company implement video teleconferencing successfully within its organization. We sought out companies with positive video teleconferencing experiences and invited their leaders to impart to others the practical lessons they learned in the course of their work.

The Information Age has brought with it the need to concern ourselves with man-machine interactions. Systems must be designed to be "human-friendly;" man-machine dialogs must be efficient and easy to master. Telecommunications technology is at the heart of these dialogs — allowing us, from the comfort of our offices and homes, to pay bills, order merchandise, make reservations, execute trades on the floors of the securities markets, and to become informed by accessing vast remote data bases. All this would be unthinkable without telecommunications.

Video teleconferencing is similarly an application of telecommunications technology. Yet, while other advances in telecommunications have made *man-machine* interactions simpler and more efficient, video teleconferencing can make *man-to-man* interactions more productive. Take a moment to ponder the importance of that statement. Distance which previously inhibited the timely conduct of face-to-face and graphics interaction can be overcome electronically. Valuable time can be saved and decisions expedited — and perhaps even improved — because the trip which otherwise would be postponed will be supplanted by an electronic meeting that can be conducted immediately.

Dramatic advances have become so familiar to us. Our world economy is spawning technologies so quickly that some companies are able to achieve unheard-of-successes in their first year of existence while more established companies cannot adapt as quickly to the changing times. Product life cycles are undergoing dramatic reductions. In Chapter 4, John Hart of Gould Incorporated provides a striking illustration of the importance of mobilizing your organization to react more swiftly in a rapidly changing environment. More frequent and more efficient communications is the order of the day.

If you lift your gaze above the pile of reports, correspondence, and mail that accumulated during your last business trip, you may see a future in which a distant face-to-face meeting does not mean that you will fall behind in your work. We see that day coming quickly. It is likely you do, too.

PREFACE

The Executive Guide to Video Teleconferencing is a book written by non-technical managers about an exciting innovation which they have helped to successfully introduce to their organizations — live, interactive conferences and meetings conducted by way of closed circuit video facilities. This process, known as video teleconferencing, consists of ordinary people, telecommunications technology, and video studio facilities which, when integrated into a system, result in higher productivity, reduced travel time and expense, and greater communication.

The book is a collection of contributions from governmental, medical, and commercial organizations which have taken leading roles in the application of technology to a common problem — time lost to unproductive meetings and consultations. Each of the authors provides a unique point of view and application, making the book provocative and informative.

The targeted audience for the book is the executive or administrator responsible for improving productivity and communications, although project members concerned with the same goal will also be interested.

Aetna Life and Casualty writes about its experiences using video teleconferencing in the greater Hartford area. While most early users of video teleconferencing tried to cut down on long distance meetings, Aetna realized that a considerable amount of time was also being wasted attending meetings across-town. Aetna describes how it created a task force to study the problem and to implement the chosen solution.

Gould, Inc., a $2 billion company engaged in all phases of high technology, relates how it is constructing its own internal communications and video teleconferencing network, "Gouldnet." Gould's Director of Corporate Telecommunications explains how and why the company has entered a period of transition from an industrial products producer to an electronic products manufacturer.

The author explains the changes required in the organization and its ability to respond rapidly to change as the product life cycle drops from 10-20 years in industrial products to 18-36 months in electronic products. He explains why video telecommunication teleconferencing is the key to meeting the challenge, and how Gould is introducing a new meeting service for its engineering staff which is situated in cities throughout the USA.

The government of Ontario, Canada, explains why it identified video teleconferencing as the key to providing the same level of services in the northern half of the province that is available in the southern region. The government routinely employs consultants and specialists in a variety of health care and other social services who travel the province providing support and expert advice to local staff in their respective areas of specialization. The government found it was often faced with unfilled jobs in many professional positions because of the reluctance of skilled individuals to relocate to the "isolated" north.

Additionally, the regional and district offices of decentralized ministries need to meet with head-office staff — traditionally accomplished by face-to-face meetings requiring travel to headquarters. Video teleconferencing is solving this problem for the government of Ontario, and the project supervisor explains how the government successfully employed the new meeting tool.

The West Virginia Research and Training Center (WVR&TC) is a federally funded organization whose responsibility is to provide training on a national basis to professionals in Vocational Rehabilitation. Live training, requiring a considerable budget, is their stock-in-trade. The authors describe how a national private network was created and how it is used to deliver the live training sessions. Citing specific costs and cost considerations, they take a detailed look at successfully organizing the project.

Medical Care Development (MCD) is an organization devoted to the identification and resolution of problems in health care delivery in Maine. MCD recognized that travel throughout Aroostook County in northern Maine, was quite time consuming and that participation by Aroostook health care professionals in frequent meetings and educational activities had to be simplified. Furthermore, a survey conducted by MCD indicated that professional isolation in the rural areas was the most commonly cited problem for rural health care problem and reports on its specific experiences with education, training, and meetings.

Greater Southeast Community Hospital reveals how video teleconferencing is employed by radiologists to reduce the time required to have emergency room computerized tomography and nuclear medicine scans reviewed remotely by the most qualified on-call radiologists during eh hours from 11:00 p.m. to 8:00 a.m. During the course of the past three years, the new technology, which they call "teleradiology," has benefited nearly 1,000 patients.

In the opening chapter, a market review for teleconferencing is given. The various forms of teleconferencing technology and systems are discussed to provide the reader with a firm grasp of the field. An analysis of recent trends is provided as are the reasons each of the teleconferencing methods is used.

ACKNOWLEDGEMENTS

We are indebted to the contributing authors for sharing with us their keen professional insight and understanding. Their contributions make this book relevant and real. We are grateful, as well, to their organizations which, having assumed the risk of an exciting new venture, have permitted their video teleconferencing managers and engineers to devote time to this important book.

We heartily thank our colleaques at First Communications Group, Inc. whose timely suggestions, help, and patience helped us to maintain our course. Special thanks are extended to Robert Howard for his foresight and support.

FIRST COMMUNICATIONS GROUP, INC.

A comprehensive overview is provided of the driving forces which have propelled video teleconferencing to the forefront. Video teleconferencing is defined and contrasted with alternative forms of teleconferencing. Specific case studies are referred to for each form of teleconferencing. This chapter quickly brings the reader up-to-date on the state of the art and the future of video teleconferencing.

Chapter 1
Video Teleconferencing:
A Market, Trend and Technology Review
Dr. Ronald J. Bohm

Video teleconferencing is not new. It has been technically feasible for more than a decade and has been economically feasible in some forms since the mid-1970s. Why, therefore, is it just emerging, twenty years after the introduction of the ill-fated Picture-Phone* demonstrated at the New York World's Fair?

Cost is certainly a consideration. The high cost of full-motion video conferencing systems (complete with color transmission capabilities, high resolution graphics monitors, and high speed, and high definition intelligent copiers or facsimile units) has been the major reason for the slow development of the video teleconferencing market. But other factors have inhibited the development and acceptance of video teleconferencing. These factors include:

- Malfunctioning equipment;
- Obtrusive equipment designs;
- Lack of satellite capacity; and
- Difficulties in establishing multi-site and intercompany communications.

Early users of video teleconferencing technology expected the quality of the video to equal broadcast television. They were disappointed to find distortion caused by normal body movements. The excitement surrounding the new gadgetry led some organizations to sell the technology (the "sizzle") when they should have been selling the process and its benefits (the "steak"). Predictably, this common

---

*A trademark of American Telephone & Telegraph.

error resulted in a heartfelt longing in many pioneers for face-to-face meetings and a chance to get away from the office for a few days.

The limitations of the technology were not readily soluble, so the meeting format and style were required to change to suit the technical limitations. Unfortunately, attendees were inhibited by the intrusion and meeting effectiveness was adversely affected.

Those who employed less ambitious teleconferencing technologies (such as stop-action video and audiographic teleconferencing) ran into fewer problems as participants had lower expectations of the systems and were more willing to adapt to the circumstances of the meeting. Others experimented with various forms of video teleconferencing by starting with special event teleconferencing (also known as *ad hoc* teleconferencing) to gain some experience of their own under the auspices of a special events "producer" who provided the equipment, transmission facilities, and experience.

The newest systems have been designed to overcome these barriers. Production and communications equipment have been redesigned with more redundancy to reduce the agonizing delays caused by "technical difficulties" which result in lost interest. Video teleconferencing rooms have been redesigned to hide the studio equipment. Microphones are available in recessed cabinets and meeting rooms are made to resemble ordinary conference rooms. Satellite capacity is no longer scarce and multi-site conferences can be arranged through a network of agents and brokers.

BENEFITS OF TELECONFERENCING

In a Satellite Business Systems study, researchers were startled to find that the average elapsed time between the perceived need for a meeting and the actual date of the meeting was 47 days. Perhaps one reason for this failure to get together is the complexity of coordinating the calendars of traveling personnel. With any of the forms of teleconferencing, there is really no need to postpone an important meeting until all of the parties can be in the same city with one another. Key people located in remote areas can now be called upon to participate in company activities that could not be justified with conventional travel. Consequently, decisions can be made sooner with less disruption to normal operations and less uncertainty.

Teleconferencing is an excellent way to "gather the troops," whether for a routine product kickoff, the announcement of new policies or programs, or mobilization in times of crisis. It makes it possible for a greater number of people to become involved in project and task force work, which can produce a greater feeling of participation within the organization.

Teleconferencing not only decreases the lead time for meetings, it also tends to make the meetings more effective. A teleconference requires more planning than an "in person" meeting; consequently, shorter and more effective meetings are usually the result. Since personnel in two or more cities must be prepared for the meeting, more attention is devoted to the preparation of agendas, handouts, and presentation media. Less time is spent socializing because meetings are held more frequently with more accomplished in each meeting. In some cases, the use of long distance transmission seems to reduce the urge to waste time with small talk.

TRENDS INFLUENCING THE ACCEPTANCE OF VIDEO TELECONFERENCING

Video teleconferencing is frequently thought to be mostly applicable to executive meetings because of the high cost of executive travel and the difficulty of coordinating busy schedules. In truth, the uses of video teleconferencing are many and varied. For example, video teleconferencing has been used to facilitate job interviews with little loss of personal contact.

In recent years, a growing number of firms have moved away from the traditional pyramid organization to a matrix where job functions are less clear. The need for frequent meetings is greater as decisions are made not by individuals but by groups of peers.

In a parallel development, the adoption by many companies of the "quality circle," a quality control methodology, has created additional impetus for more frequent meetings. The fact that engineering and production facilities are sometimes fragmented across the country, and often among a number of sub-contractors, is having a bearing on the broader interest in video teleconferencing.

The short-term project team is yet another development increasing the need for effective communications. Usually operating under short lead times to complete projects requiring a high degree of coordination and cooperation, the project team is a natural candidate for video teleconferencing.

Each of these trends increases the need for face-to-face or, at least, visual interaction. Given the impact of increased travel budgets,

many companies will begin to experiment with video teleconferencing.

VIDEO TELECONFERENCING
AS A SUBSTITUTE FOR TRAVEL

According to Coopers and Lybrand, the "Big Eight" accounting
firm, approximately twenty million meetings are held every day in
the United States. Of course not all of these meetings are associated
with travel or long distance communications. Quantum Science, a
New York research firm, estimates that in 1981 only 90,000 meetings
were conducted using some form of teleconferencing in their organizations, Coopers and Lybrand estimates that travel costs are cut by
15% to 20%. The attendee's desire to travel, and the fact that some
meetings just cannot be conducted as effectively at a distance, are
offered as explanations for this respectable, but not overpowering,
percentage.

Research has shown, however, that some business travelers would
be receptive to reduced travel. A Bell Canada study indicates that of
those who travel at least 15 times per year, 45% would prefer fewer
trips, while only 16% of those who traveled 5 times per year would
want to cut back. That is, it is the heavy traveler who will be inclined
to use video teleconferencing.

Separate studies by the University of California and AT&T estimated that 75% of business travel is for meetings, while 60% of those
trips (or 45% of all travel for business meetings), are intracompany.
If only half of those intracompany trips could be conducted electronically, it is clear how more than 20% of business travel could be
eliminated. The Coopers and Lybrand estimate correlates with this
reasoning.

THE TYPES OF VIDEO TELECONFERENCING
AND OTHER ALTERNATIVES

While the main focus of this book is the implementation of video
teleconferencing and its applications, the discussion would not be
complete without reviewing the different types of video teleconferencing and the alternatives to video. Video teleconferencing, as used
in this book, includes full-motion (usually one-way) video, compressed full-motion video, and audiographic teleconferencing.
There are two other prominent teleconferencing methods: audio
teleconferencing and computer conferencing.

FULL-MOTION VIDEO TELECONFERENCING

Full-motion video teleconferencing is rarely used for two-way interactive video applications because it requires a large bandwidth (channel size) and it is prohibitively expensive except for broadcast (point-to-multipoint) and commercial television applications. In a typical one-way full-motion video teleconference, the video program is transmitted from a single site, usually a television studio (or hotel) with commercial quality editing and production equipment. The presenters address a number of remote participants in other cities who typically receive the video signal via satellite. A return audio channel is often present in the receiving sites to allow the viewers to direct questions to the presenters or to other viewers at other receiving locations.

Naturally, the problem of simultaneous use of the audio channel must be controlled so that only one remote participant at a time can address the presenter or another remote participant. This control is achieved by using an audio bridge — a device which uses various methods to select one of a number of contending parties requesting to use the channel.

Most users of one-way full-motion video teleconferencing use it infrequently because of the effort and expense involved. Hence, one-way full-motion video teleconferencing is usually referred to as special event or ad hoc video teleconferencing.

Users of Full-Motion Video Teleconferencing

Duke University Medical Center. Physicians participating in a nationwide satellite network at Duke University Medical Center in Durham, North Carolina keep on top of the latest medical research and learn the newest forms of patient care techniques without leaving the hospital. The in-hospital viewing capability offered by the satellite-fed communications system allows doctors to attend more of these sessions than would otherwise be possible.

The State of Alaska. The State of Alaska has been using video teleconferencing since 1978 to link the state legislature with statewide information offices. The distances between cities and the rough terrain made video teleconferencing a natural solution for the state.

The Ford Motor Company. Ford Motor Company introduced its 1981 EXP and LN7 sport coupes to more than 20,000 dealers and sales personnel in 38 cities in what was then the largest special event teleconference ever conducted. The video portion of the event included two live 90-minute segments during the day, and a one-hour press conference in the evening. Ford has since conducted three other satellite teleconferences.

Merrill Lynch & Co., Inc. Merrill Lynch, the largest securities and brokerage firm in the United States, used a satellite video teleconference in 1981 to present a seminar on a newly enacted tax law change to their brokers and their clients in 30 cities around the country. Two months later, the brokerage firm again used satellite video teleconferencing for another seminar. In November 1982, they conducted a 12,000-participant satellite meeting in 30 cities, using the facilities of a hotel ballroom in each location.

The Bank Administration Institute. The Bank Administration Institute held a satellite video teleconference to educate 4,000 bankers in the implications of the newly approved bank-offered money market certificates of deposit. The program participants paid $95 each for the four-hour seminar. Many financial analysts have remarked that banks never needed to be so responsive to change before, and that new technologies will be required for quickly adapting. Certainly, the use of satellite video teleconferencing was one such technological tool.

NET Telcon. On October 22, 1983, an estimated 25,000 investors flocked to the nearest Public Broadcasting System stations to view a pay-per-view event featuring some of the most highly respected Wall Street figures. For the privilege of participating, investors paid from $50 to $75 each to NET Telcon, a division of WNET-TV in New York. Using the same technology as is commonly used on The "MacNeil/ Lehrer Report" — on which guests appear at PBS studios around the nation and are included on a monitor in either the Washington, D.C. or New York studios — the PBS stations are uniquely equipped to offer full-motion video teleconferencing. Special effects can be incorporated into the broadcast at the modest cost of $100.

Picker Corp. Picker Corp, a medical equipment manufacturer, held a national meeting in 1974 at a cost of $420,000 for travel, lodging, and hall expenses to assemble the attendees in one place. In 1980 it used Holiday Inn's Hi-Net service to host a similar size conference at 29 locations and reduced its overall costs to $80,000, an 81% reduction!

Full-Motion Video Teleconferencing Costs

Full-motion video teleconferencing costs range from $10,000 to as much as $500,000 depending on the type of system and services used. A full service special event producer will provide pre-production assistance with slides, tapes, and speeches, multiple cameras, special lighting, and graphics. Other factors influencing the pricing include:

- Rental of receiving locations, including any portable downlinks to be used;
- The number of cities to be included with return audio;
- Satellite time;
- Uplinking, including any relays between the origination site and the uplink;
- The format of the satellite conference;
- Consultant or broker fees for program and system management and administration;
- Program planning and development;
- Rental of origination site; and
- The number and size of projection equipment needed at remote sites.

Operational Considerations

In the remainder of this section, some of the more unfamiliar considerations are explored. A comprehensive look at one organization's experience with full-motion video teleconferencing costs is provided by West Virginia Rehabilitation Research and Training Center in Chapter 8.

The Program Origination Site. A conference organizer may originate the broadcast from a television studio which has the advantage of being specifically designed for television production, thus avoiding many of the technical problems that otherwise occur.

The Uplink. The simplest way to get the video signal to the satellite or other long distance network for distribution is to have a satellite gateway at the studio site — usually in the form of a satellite earth station. The transmitting earth station typically has a diameter of 30 feet and costs $1 million or more. Although it is possible to get adjustable earth stations which can transmit to more than one satellite, the earth station is typically pointed in a fixed manner at a single satellite.

A portable uplink is another solution which may be more appealing to sporadic users of video teleconferencing. Not all locations can make use of a portable uplink, however, because of the need for a line-of-sight to the satellite with a minimum of spectral interference.

A third choice is to find a long distance carrier that will provide transmission services for your video teleconferencing. Typically, the carrier will offer shared use of an earth station satellite antenna, but you may be required to make arrangements to interconnect your studio with the earth station. This can be accomplished by one or more of several alternatives, including: the telephone company, common carrier microwave, private microwave, coaxial cable, fiber optics, or infrared lightwave.

The Downlink. Downlinks are receive-only systems which are less complex and less costly than uplinks. As with an uplink, a downlink may be either fixed or adjustable. Portable downlinks are available and are relatively easy to set up, providing a clear line-of-sight is possible.

Meeting Formats. Satellite video teleconference meetings can be designed in a number of different formats, including "one up one down," "one up many down," "two up one down," and "many up many down."

The "one up one down" format is used for one-way conferencing between offices, generally with an audio return from the downlink site to the uplink site. The "one up many down" format is for announcements, training, product releases, and other kinds of broadcast applications. The "two up two down" is a two-way video teleconference in which both sites have full-motion or compressed motion video uplink capabilities. Finally, the "many up many down" format is a complex directorial format in which more than two sites are in video teleconference with one another. The complexity arises from the need to control which video images are captured on the receive monitors. This conference mode is more expensive, and there is far less experience to report than with the other formats.

Generally, the more uplinks that are installed, the more transponders that will be required. Since a company may reserve transponder time under rental or lease arrangements, it is advantageous to make as much use of the reserved time as possible. This becomes more difficult when uplink arrangements are made in more than one site.

COMPRESSED FULL-MOTION
VIDEO TELECONFERENCING

Compressed full-motion video teleconferencing permits video teleconferencing to be employed more regularly than special event video teleconferencing. As mentioned earlier, to achieve the same full-motion quality as we are familiar with on television, a large channel is required. High telecommunications costs led to the development of the *codec* (coder/decoder) which not only codes and decodes the analog video signals produced by full-motion cameras, but also compresses the signal to reduce the overall requirement for channel size.

Compression is not normally achieved without penalty, however. Generally, the codecs use a number of algorithms to summarize unchanged portions of the picture and to predict the next image in each picture element in order to reduce channel traffic. In doing so, however, the quality of image degrades during times of rapid motion as the ability of the codec to predict the image declines.

For administrative meetings which are characterized by little motion, compressed full-motion video teleconferencing produces very acceptable quality. Even if a presenter makes a rapid head movement, the resulting picture distortion, though noticeable, is only a minor distraction since the image quality quickly reverts to normal.

Until recently, the most advanced codecs required a channel speed of 1.544 Mbps (million bits per second; a bit is the smallest unit of information and generally requires a 1 Hz bandwidth), and cost around $150,000 per end. Development is under way at several laboratories to reduce the required bandwidth even further. Perhaps the most interesting development in compressed full-motion codecs is happening at Widergren Communications, Inc. of San Jose, California.

Widergren has built a codec that interfaces to a transmission line operating at only 56 Kbps (kilobits per second). This represents a reduction in required transmission speed by a factor of 24! Compared with the 80-90 Mbps required for full-motion, the device delivers a compression of greater than 100 times. It is even more surprising that a compressed full-motion system can operate with high fidelity at the same transmission rates as some stop-action video systems.

The U.S. Defense Department's Advanced Research Projects Agency (DARPA) believes it will be possible to develop a limited-use codec for compressed full-motion video teleconferencing for use in field operations at 19.2 Kbits/s.

How can these devices achieve so much compression? According to

Widergren, it is not only what they do, but how they do it, that has permitted them to break earlier barriers. The device accepts ordinary video signals from a color TV camera or video recorder and digitizes them at 88 Mbps. They apply "spatial averaging and filtering" to reduce the bit stream to 22 Mbps. "Temporal averaging" further compresses the signal to between 2 and 3 Mbps. Another technique, known as "conditional replenishment," provides an additional tenfold reduction in the required transmission rate to a few hundred thousand bits per second. The next scheme divides each frame into blocks of eight pixels (eight-bit picture elements or dots) on a side and compares each block with the prior one to see if it has changed. If the block has not changed, it needs no transmission, allowing a further reduction. Finally, a variant of "Huffman encoding" allows for the eight-bit pixel to be reduced to one bit depending on the frequency with which that pixel is repeated.

When motion within the image occurs less than ten percent of the time, the Widergren picture quality is very good. When that threshold is exceeded, however, picture quality degrades quickly and remains that way until the level of motion falls below the threshold.

Perhaps the most striking aspect of the development of the Widergren codec is the prospect that stop-action video will be eclipsed by compressed full-motion video. At the high end, stop-action systems operate at 56 Kbps to deliver a new image once every 13 seconds. There will continue to be markets for stop-action, especially in medical imaging. However, for those who eschewed compressed full-motion video and adopted stop-action to justify more easily the entry into video teleconferencing, the economics of compressed full-motion may become compelling.

The Widergren codec will initially be priced at $85,000 per end (more than 40% less than its 1.544 Mbps counterpart) and is expected to sell for $50,000 once production volume increases. Even with a 66% reduction in codec prices, the main selling point of the 56 Kbps codec is the reduction in telecommunications costs when compared with the 1.544 Mbps devices. Twenty-four organizations can now share the same satellite transponder capacity which was formerly required for just one video teleconference!

Applications of Compressed Full-Motion Video Teleconferencing

M/A-COM, Inc. Dr. Lawrence Gould, chairman and chief executive officer of M/A-COM, uses video teleconferencing at his office in Boca Raton, Florida to oversee the 26 companies that make up the M/A-COM organization. This allows Gould to use a nine-room suite as the corporate headquarters for the large telecommunications conglomerate, although none of the operating units is located in Boca Raton. M/A-COM has four regional video teleconference centers located in San Diego, California; Catawba, North Carolina; Germantown, Maryland; and Burlington, Massachusetts. In use since 1981, M/A-COM is so pleased with the system, it is marketing it through its Macomnet subsidiary.

ARCO and Allstate Insurance. Both ARCO and Allstate Insurance are building video teleconferencing networks with enough excess capacity to sell to outside users. The heavy cost of their satellite earth station facilities and transponders has driven them into the telecommunications services business. ARCO expects to reduce its travel cost by 23% as its systems become fully operational, while Allstate expects to shave 15% off its travel expense, a savings which it feels is more than adequate to earn a rapid payback on its investment.

Boeing Co., Inc. Boeing Co., Inc. shaved 30 days off of the development time of its 757 jet airliner through the use of video teleconferencing. The investment in the video teleconferencing systems and transmission network was insignificant when compared with the savings brought about by higher workforce productivity.

Dow Chemical U.S.A. In 1974, Dow Chemical U.S.A. began a pilot program that connected researchers in Midland, Michigan and Freeport, Texas. The pilot program was halted in 1977 because of cost. In 1982, however, the availability of long-distance satellite circuits made the video teleconferencing link feasible.

Bank of America. In 1982, cost led Bank of America to temporarily abandon plans for a custom–built video teleconferencing system. Instead, the company decided to utilize an audio teleconferencing system that can link up to eight or nine people using the telephone. For its purposes, Bank of America is waiting for the cost of video teleconferencing to decline or for its need for the system to increase.

Arthur Andersen & Co. From 1977 to 1981 Arthur Andersen & Co. participated in a four year field trial of video teleconferencing arranged by AT&T. Partners of the accounting firm participated from four locations: Chicago; New York; Washington, D.C.; and San Francisco (their Geneva, Switzerland world headquarters participated by telephone only). The 4-way simultaneous video was a bold use of the technology and resulted in some predictable problems. Overall, however, the partners were very pleased and acknowledged that many of the meetings conducted using video teleconferencing could not have otherwise been arranged with conventional travel because of schedule conflicts.

Digital Equipment Corporation. Digital Equipment Corporation (DEC) expects that the savings in travel cost and increased productivity wrought by video teleconferencing will allow it to recoup its investment if the facilities are used 80% of the time. DEC uses the system heavily within Massachusetts, sometimes over distances shorter than 30 miles.

Compressed Full-Motion Video Teleconferencing Costs

Some of the costs of compressed full-motion video teleconferencing have already been discussed in this chapter, especially the economics of codecs. But the codecs are just one of many components. A fully equipped full-motion video teleconference room can easily cost more than $1 million excluding the cost of the telecommunications facilities.

The telecommunications costs are also steep. For example, users of AT&T's Picturephone Meeting Service (PMS) — an in-house video teleconferencing facility supplied and supported by AT&T — pay $1,640 per hour for a meeting held between New York and Los Angeles. Users of AT&T's 13 public PMS meeting rooms pay nearly twice that amount.

For those organizations that find they need the benefits of compressed full-motion over stop-action video, it is not necessary to build a first class meeting room for $1 million. More modest facilities can be designed and installed for $250 thousand including the $150 thousand for the 1.544 Mbps codec. With the advent of the Widergren codec, these rooms can be installed for $185 thousand. If the room can be heavily utilized, it is very possible your organization might soon be evaluating compressed full-motion video teleconferencing.

AUDIOGRAPHIC TELECONFERENCING

Audiographic teleconferencing will be the fastest growing teleconferencing method during the mid-1980s. The primary services incorporated into audiographic teleconferences are stop-action video, telewriting, facsimile, and remote slide projectors. While some would classify stop-action video as a special case of full-motion video teleconferencing, it is classified here as audiographic only because the applications of stop-action video are most similar to those of audiographic conferences. Telewriting simply means transmission of handwriting from one location to another using electronic blackboards or electronic tablets. Facsimile is the scanning of documents and the transmission of the resulting signals. Remote slide projectors are ordinary slide projectors which are controlled from the central audiographic site by the meeting manager.

Stop-Action Video Teleconferencing

Stop-action video teleconferencing is to full-motion video teleconferencing what snapshots are to movies. A single picture is recorded at an originating site and is transmitted, usually along voice-grade telephone lines, to a destination where a video monitor displays the image.

Stop-action, also known as freeze-frame or slow-scan, is not applicable to all situations because of the distraction of a slowly changing video image. This concept is most useful when a single image — be it a drawing, graph, or body scan — must be observed remotely in short order. But in a face-to-face meeting of managers or in a sales presentation meeting, it would not be as effective as full-motion or compressed full-motion video teleconferencing.

When cost considerations are taken into effect, however, some will choose stop-action even with the lower time-effectiveness of the medium. An excellent description of the technical considerations of stop-action systems is given in Chapter 5.

Users of Stop-Action Video Teleconferencing

Westinghouse Electric Corp. Westinghouse Electric Corp. was dissatisfied with the lack of standards in the industry for the codecs (coder/decoders) which convert video signals to digital streams (see the discussion on codecs in the section on compressed full-motion video teleconferencing above). By waiting for standardization, Westinghouse hopes to be able to video teleconference with other companies using a variety of codecs. As an interim step, Westinghouse is using a stop-action video teleconferencing system.

International Business Machines (IBM). IBM uses its slow scan video teleconferencing system to support manufacturing and design groups. Developers of a new product are linked using black-and-white stop-action video with the initial systems having two monitors in each room — one for graphics and one for people. The people monitor is used at the beginning of the meeting to allow the participants to see who they are meeting with. After the preliminary introductions, the primary focal point is the graphics monitor. After a 1979 pilot project proved successful, IBM expanded its network to 35 rooms by the end of 1982.

Stop-Action Video Teleconferencing Costs

A black-and-white stop-action system can be installed for as little as $10,000, while a color stop-action system can be purchased for just $14,000. The rooms can be ordinary or as posh as some corporate compressed full-motion video teleconferencing rooms. Optional equipment and facilities can bring the cost up near $50,000 by including high resolution color cameras and monitors. But for most applications, the low-end systems are more than adequate.

For more detailed information on budgeting for a stop-action video teleconferencing system, see Chapter 6.

Telewriting

Telewriting is ideal for interactive discussions where the ideas being conveyed are more important than the facial expressions and body language of the communicators.

With the electronic blackboard, an image, written or drawn with regular chalk on the blackboard, is sensed by a pressure sensitive grid, digitized and transmitted to another conference location where it is displayed on a monitor. A second telephone line is usually utilized for a simultaneous voice conversation.

AT&T Information Systems's Gemini 100 may be installed at a monthly cost of around $800 per location for both sending and receiving capabilities. For infrequent use, the Gemini 100 costs about $66 per hour to use, a price which is well within reach of most companies.

As an alternative to the Gemini 100, one may use a tablet and stylus rather than a chalkboard. These are generally smaller and, therefore, are more portable than Gemini 100. The Telewriter II, offered by Optel Communications, Inc. of New York, allows the conferees to manipulate up to 15 pages of erasable memory. By manipulating the Telewriter II controller's 14 buttons, the user can switch between two colors, manipulate a pointer, and selectively erase or clear the screen. These functions are above and beyond the Gemini 100's capabilities and can be added to the audiographic conference room for around $9,000 for the basic system.

Facsimile

A popular and well known tool for any kind of teleconference is the facsimile transmission of documents and graphics. Users of facsimile use one of four CCITT (Consultative Committee on International Telephone and Telegraph) standard protocols for transmission. Groups I and II allow documents to be transmitted at the rate of from 1 to 6 minutes per page depending on the speed of the *modem* (modulator-demodulator) being used to interface to the voice-grade telephone lines. Group III users can transmit documents in less than a minute while the new Group IV standard expected to be approved soon, would move a page in a few seconds. It is easy to see how a subminute device can facilitate the conduct of a teleconference, whether it be a full-motion video or an audio teleconference. Group III facsimile equipment can be purchased for around $4,500 per site and transfers documents at the rate of one page every 45 seconds.

Remote Slide Projectors

Remote slide and microfiche projectors help to create a familiar presentation format during a teleconference. Not only can the attendees hear the speaker's voice, but they also can view the presentation media just as if the presenter were in the conference room. Random access controllers allow the presenter to operate controls on the conference bridge equipment and to select slides for projection without going in a serial fashion. This is especially helpful during question and answer sessions following the presentation.

In a multi-location audiographic teleconference, all of the remote locations would simultaneously view the same slides or fiche. At roughly $900 per site, remote slide projection is an excellent addition to an audiographic conference room.

AUDIO TELECONFERENCING

Audio teleconferencing is the most familiar of teleconferencing techniques. From the use of speakerphones to the more complicated conference call, the audio conference is the least costly way to bring large numbers of participants together in a conference with little in-house equipment or preparation. Studies have indicated that as many as 85% of the interactions done face-to-face can take place via telephone conferencing, with no loss of effectiveness.

The strengths of audio teleconferencing include the following points:

- The telephone is the most readily available and most widely understood means for teleconferencing;

- There are 400,000,000 telephones installed around the world;

- Teleconferences can be arranged with very little notice, planning, or preparation;

- Compared to other teleconferencing methods, it can be relatively inexpensive to use if properly managed.

Audio teleconferences may use ordinary dial-up facilities or dedicated lines. The latter is less common, but when heavy utilization is made of the facilities it becomes economically attractive and simplifies the access to the conference — all that needs to be done is pick up the phone and the conference can begin. Dedicated lines can become a constraint, however, because they are not available in homes, hotel rooms, or other sites in which widely dispersed participants might be found.

Typically, an in-house audio teleconference is preplanned to be held at a given hour. In dial-up audio teleconferences, a time is established for the remote participants to place an ordinary phone call to the central site. A dial-up audio teleconference may be arranged through a telephone company conference operator, or through the use of sophisticated bridging equipment at the central site to interconnect all the callers into what is called a "meet-me" audio teleconference.

In an operator assisted audio teleconference, the central site arranges with the telephone company operator to call all of the remote participants at the given hour. The operator assisted conference call suffers from a number of flaws which become more pronounced when the number of remote locations gets above five to seven. The most significant problem is the difficulty of getting all the parties on their phones at the same time. Some participants must be lined up early, and waits of more than five minutes to complete the circuit can be damaging to the conference. Noise levels increase as remote sites are added, and the distance between the remote sites and the central site can affect the sound level heard at either end.

Equally difficult is the problem of managing the meeting since, theoretically, everyone "has the floor." A meeting manager must be appointed to "recognize" speakers in some organized fashion to reduce (but rarely eliminate) crosstalk.

to discuss the plant managers' budgets. Now, the area administrative offices are equipped with audio teleconference equipment to interact with the Houston headquarters. What was expected to take five hours of teleconferencing, was accomplished in half that time.

The oil company is waiting for the bandwidth requirements of compressed full-motion video teleconferencing to decline. When it does, they will take another evolutionary step.

Audio Teleconferencing Costs

As a rule of thumb, an audio teleconference will cost between $20 and $40 per hour per location plus equipment rental, if any. Bridges are available from $500 to $2,500 per port (one-port interfaces with one telephone line) depending on the level of sophistication. A remote conference room can be equipped with audio conference conveners for $1,000 to $2,000.

COMPUTER CONFERENCING

Computer conferencing is the least familiar form of teleconferencing since the meetings are held over a long period of time with each participant making his contribution to the conference in the privacy of his home or office according to his own time schedule. A strange cross between a meeting, a correspondence, and a bulletin board, computer conferencing is becoming increasingly popular as personal and home computers abound.

In a computer conference, a conference manager uses the computer to notify the "attendees" of an upcoming agenda. The attendees return their comments to the manager to finalize the agenda. The manager will typically ask the participants to prepare statements on the individual agenda items. The submissions made during the computer conference are deposited into a single computer file, but the messages are tagged with the names or account numbers of the recipients. By assigning group account codes, a sender can tag a message with the group code and the message will be made available to all of the group's members.

The beauty of a computer conference is that it does not require simultaneous participation. Hours or weeks may elapse between the beginning and the end of a computer conference. Participants may prepare their material in their own time and in their own offices.

Time zone differences are another problem that is solved by computer conferencing. Since the recipients are not bound by the confines of their office, conference material may be retrieved at home, while traveling, and not necessarily during office hours.

Using a well designed computer conference system, respondents can use "notes mode" to apply their comments to a message they received so that the notes are highlighted when the message is passed back to the originator. Another unique property of a computer conference is that all correspondence is in written form and may be stored in document files on the computer. Hard copy records are available at the touch of a button and the power of the computer can be used to search the text of a conference, edit the proceedings, and otherwise process the material.

Computer conferencing is one of the lowest cost conferencing methods because it does not require prime-time transmission facilities. Long distance lines which are busy during office hours can be used after hours for batch movement of conference material from one computer to another.

Furthermore, no special meeting skills are necessary beyond the ability to operate a keyboard terminal and to prepare written material. Some managers have their secretaries perform the actual entry and retrieval of the messages.

Computer conferencing is held by some to be the optimal method of conducting forecasting by the Delphi technique, a methodology developed by the Rand Corporation of Santa Monica. When using the Delphi method, experts anonymously share opinions over the course of several rounds. For example, in the first round, the participants might each submit their view of potential political, economic, social, and cultural impacts on the future.

By using computer conferencing, each participant would receive these position papers and could respond anonymously without prejudice to the parties who have created them. In this way, at least in theory, the pure ideas stand a better chance of being reviewed for their own merit without the complications of ego. The Delphi method allows for the "discussion" to continue until a consensus is reached by the participants. With computer conferencing, even the longest of Delphi sessions would be handled easily since the participants could make their individual contributions asynchronously according to their own schedules.

Computer Conferencing Systems and Applications

Notepad. Notepad, the product of the San Bruno, California-based Infomedia Corp., is a menu-driven computer conference system which is available by the hour via Tymnet, a public access value-added network, or in-house on any Digital Equipment computer supporting the Tops-20 operating system. The cost per hour is $67 and the in-house version costs·$50,000.

The system is used by 400 individuals from 65 utility companies licensed to build or operate nuclear reactor power generating plants. As a result of the Three Mile Island near-disaster, the special investigating commission recommended the exchange of information between plant operators and designers to avoid other incidents. It is not unusual for 20 or more individual conferences to be simultaneously conducted by the nuclear group.

Genie. Genie (General Information Environment) is the product of Portland, Oregon-based Data Dynamics. Genie combines the facilities of computer conferencing and a relational data base management system. So interrelated are the two that Genie conferences are called "repositories" which are organized by an administrator who has general editing responsibilities. Other valuable features of Genie include communications, word and graphics processing, calendar management, scheduling functions, and a personal information management system.

Genie operates either under the highly portable Unix operating system or on the Control Data Cyber 175 mainframe computer. The mainframe version sells for $65,000 while the Unix version for minicomputers is available for $35,000.

The Electronic Information Exchange System (EIES). The EIES network is offered by the New Jersey Institute of Technology as an experimental testing ground for those wishing to get experience in computer conferencing. EIES has a large user population consisting of sociologists and computer scientists who have studied the system while also being users themselves.

EIES offers a rich set of conferencing utilities which can be used in a limited fashion to foster learning. Included are tree-structured menus and an on-line operator to help solve nearly all user difficulties with the system. The system monitors all usage and prepares elaborate management reports to users. EIES keeps track of who has seen which text so a sender always can obtain an acknowledgement of receipt.

Matrix Transaction Exchange (Matrix). Matrix is the offering of Cross Information Co. of Boulder, Colorado. The distinguishing characteristic of Matrix is its provision for administrative control of the computer conference by the Matrix system operator, conference manager, and discussion leader. A meeting status indicator is used to permit participants to quickly determine the stage of the conference and, if necessary, to review any one or more of the sessions which had been concluded earlier in the proceedings.

Matrix is available on a monthly lease for $1,000 for DEC systems, or for $25 per hour on a time shared computer.

THE AUTHOR

Dr. Ronald J. Bohm is President of First Communications Group, Inc., a company offering digital microwave telecommunications services in the intracity area for video teleconferencing, data, and voice applications. Dr. Bohm has previously served Knight Ridder Newspapers, Inc.; the Irving Trust Bank; and Playboy Enterprises, Inc. in a variety of systems, communications, and marketing roles. He is a contributing author to *Teleconferencing and Interactive Media '84* (University of Wisconsin-Extension, Center for Interactive Programs, Madison, Wisconsin 1984), *APL In Practice* (John Wiley & Sons, New York, 1980), and he speaks frequently before telecommunications and management information systems audiences.

Dr. Bohm received his Ph.D. from Massachusetts Institute of Technology in 1972 for his work in Management Science as an NDEA Fellow. He earned the S.M. in Management in 1970 from the Sloan School of Management at MIT for his work in finance and economics. Dr. Bohm also holds the S.B. in Mathematics from MIT, which he received in 1968.

Ministry of Government Services

Ontario

Mrs. Biswas writes of her experiences implementing compressed two-way full-motion video teleconferencing for the Government of Ontario. She explains how the geography of the province of Ontario necessitated the use of telecommunications technology to fulfill a social need. This case study provides a wealth of detailed information on the design and implementation of a video teleconferencing network.

Chapter 2
The Government of Ontario Teleconference Service
Neeru M. Biswas
Supervisor, Systems Development
Telecommunication Services Branch
Ministry of Government Services

BACKGROUND

The Province of Ontario, Canada, extends over 413,000 square miles — from Hudson's Bay to the north, to the border with the United States to the south — and touches the boundaries of Minnesota, Michigan, Ohio, Pennsylvania, and New York. On the east and west it borders respectively with the Canadian provinces of Quebec and Manitoba. Ontario has a population of 8.6 million. A majority lives within 100 miles of the US border, especially south of Lake Huron, and more than 3 million people live in metropolitan Toronto. The north of the province is sparsely populated, interspersed with thousands of lakes, and is richly forested. Northern residents live in small, and often geographically isolated, communities. The northern communities also witness a large and highly mobile population of visitors throughout the year — campers, skiers, hunters, and sport fishing enthusiasts.

The Government of Ontario is responsible for maintaining communication, transportation, police patrol, and for providing a variety of other services throughout the province. Furthermore, the quality of the services must be consistent throughout the province. The delivery of high quality services to the north is exceptionally challenging because of the factors described above. Many departments of the Government of Ontario (called "ministries") are geographically dispersed, as well as decentralized to be closer to the communities they serve. Regional offices are established in the larger population centres of the province (Toronto, being the provincial capital, serves as headquarters) while district, area, and local offices are set up to cover the small townships and villages that dot the province (see Figure 2-1). Headquarters are more than 1,000 miles away for many of these offices.

The Ministry of Government Services (MGS) is responsible for providing "corporate" services to the 23 ministries of the provincial government. Thus, MGS caters to the office space and related requirements of approximately 70,000 people that the province em-

Fig. 2-1 Province of Ontario (area 413,000 square miles) major population centres and some northern townships.

ploys, and handles employee data, retirement benefits, internal mail, computer services, telecommunication services, information services for public access to the government, and so on. The Telecommunications Services Branch (TSB) of the ministry, with a current operating budget of about 35 million Canadian dollars, is responsible for provisioning telecommunication services to meet effectively all the communication needs of Ontario government ministries and its agencies.

The Need for Teleconference Services

The province is committed to providing the same level of services in the north as are readily available in the south. As a result, there is great emphasis on looking for innovative and cost-effective ways to deliver timely services to the north. This provided the impetus for TSB to become involved in teleconferencing in the early 1970s.

At that time, consultants and specialists in a variety of health care and other service areas routinely traveled around the province, providing support and expert advice to local staffs in their respective areas of specialization. The government was often faced with unfilled job vacancies in many professional areas due to the reluctance of skilled individuals to relocate to the "isolated" north, despite the attraction of significant salary differentials. Coupled with this was the need for regional and district offices of decentralized ministries to meet with head-office staff — traditionally done through face-to-face meetings and usually involving travel to headquarters.

The third factor that contributed to the need for teleconferencing services was the problem of isolation experienced by some northern taxpayers and the government's determination to help alleviate that situation.

Overview

This chapter, with an emphasis on systems selection and development criteria, service implementation, promotion, applications — expected and "new" — user training, and operational service management, reviews the approach to teleconferencing that was adopted by the Government of Ontario. An effort has been made, throughout the following sections, to emphasize why a particular option was chosen over others, the lessons that were learned as the system progressed from the developmental to the operational stage, and the factors in its success.

SYSTEM DEVELOPMENT

The Telecommunications Services Branch, Ministry of Government Services, adopted an "evolutionary" approach to teleconferencing when it first looked at the concept in the mid-1970s. The concept was relatively new and not widely known or understood. A ready market did not exist for the product called "teleconferencing."

Rather than sink large amounts of capital into new, television studio-type facilities, the approach was to try out the concept through a simple, but functional, set-up of full motion video teleconferencing along with audio teleconferencing as an alternative.

Relevant literature existing at that time was searched, and existing teleconference systems within Canada were examined. A pilot system was established to evaluate various system parameters such as transmission media and networking, terminal equipment and design, teleconference room set-up and design, human factors, applications, and demand for service.

The other major decision that affected system development was that demonstrations of teleconferencing were made to potential users so they could identify their respective program areas where the benefits of teleconferencing could be realized. This method proved to be more effective than doing a needs analysis by surveying prospective users who were virtually unaware of the concept of teleconferencing.

Video teleconferencing was demonstrated and offered to potential users right from the start. It was thought that it would be easier for people unfamiliar with teleconferencing to relate to video teleconferencing, where the remote parties were still visible, rather than to audio teleconferencing which lacks the personal touch of a face-to-face meeting. Video teleconferencing also needed the least amount of training, and would be less inhibiting for a first-time participant.

System Design

System design is examined under the following headings:

- Applications
- Human Factors
- Technical Considerations
- Administrative Considerations
- Resource Requirements

Applications. Before teleconference facilities planners embark on the design of a teleconference system, it is of paramount importance that they define well the range of applications. Of course, new applications will emerge as the system develops and becomes fully operational; but, in order to plan the system initially, currently known applications must be clearly identified. The range of applications and the corresponding requirements will define the broad parameters. Once the need for teleconference services within an organization has been established, answers to questions like those listed below will be required at the outset:

- Will the teleconference facility be used primarily for business meetings such as project planning, design discussion, budgets, *et cetera?*
- Who will use the service — executives, middle management, professionals, or all?
- Will there be seminars and other educational applications?
- What will be the maximum number of people in a teleconference room?
- How much usage can be expected (e.g., 5 hours per month or 5 hours per day)?
- What visual support methods will be used (e.g., 35mm slides, chalkboard, pad board, overhead, *et cetera*)?
- Will video tapes be used for certain meetings? Will these tapes be available at each teleconference site or will one tape be used for local and remote viewing?
- Will the meeting minutes consist of a videotape recording of the meeting?
- Will personnel interviews or other meetings of a more sensitive nature be conducted using teleconferencing? What level of security will be required?
- Will there be a need to communicate with outside organizations, domestic or foreign?
- Will there be a need for linking up more than two locations at a time?

Other questions relating more to corporate culture will need to be answered as well. Planners will need to know what system capabilities will "sell" in their organization. If applications research indicates that an audiographic teleconference network will be appropriate, will it be acceptable, or will the "glamour" of full-motion video be needed to get the executive to endorse the service?

The particular organization will dictate whether a new teleconference centre will be constructed, or whether one or more of the existing meeting rooms will be upgraded to provide teleconferencing adequately. Will there be a need to present live, on-site teleconferences of events taking place all around the organization, or will all teleconferences originate from designated centres? The answer to that question will further clarify whether a fixed or transportable teleconference system will be required. Corporate culture will also help identify the need for user controlled or remote technician controlled equipment.

Human Factors. It has been said that "technology alone does not a teleconference make." Indeed, attention to ergonomic details will go a long way in making a new teleconference system a powerful and well utilized management tool in any organization.

User Friendliness. Teleconferences are basically an electronic substitute for face-to-face meetings. The ideal teleconference system, then, should be fully transparent to the participant; that is, he or she should not be aware of being in a teleconference. The least amount of change in business habits would be required which, in turn, will prove the least inhibiting for the participant.

We define user-friendliness as the degree of transparency of the system — the more transparent the system, the more userfriendly it is.

Several factors influence the user-friendliness of a system.

- The equipment should be as unobtrusive as possible. Large microphones, video cameras, and accessories all create an unfamiliar setting for a meeting. If the facility is fixed, the cameras, monitors, *et cetera*, should be recessed into the walls. A transportable, or mobile, system should be finished to match, as much as possible, the furnishings of the room in which it will be used.

- Control of the equipment should be simple to master. It should be fully automatic or remotely controlled. Control panels similar to those found in TV studios make users uncomfortable and distract them during a meeting.

- The audio sub-system should not be cumbersome or awkward. Ideally, it should be such that the user will have to do nothing specifically to activate it each time he/she wishes to speak. For free verbal interaction between participants, an "open micro-phone" system — i.e., one where microphones are always on — would be the most desirable. However, technical difficulties, such as potential for audio feedback and practical limitations (e.g., keeping several open microphones appropriately balanced through one audio mixer) may necessitate the use of push-to-talk microphones. The push-to-talk mechanism should be a simple one. We found a bar push-to-talk switch was preferred to a button or toggle type.

- The quality of the audio signal should be maintained at a high standard. It is important that the intonations of a speaker's voice are conveyed over the transmission medium. This can be done very adequately on a properly implemented voice-grade or, at best, a 5 kHz audio channel — high fidelity FM-type audio chan-nels are not required. Poor quality audio with low levels, breaks, or noise easily diverts the attention of users, causes them fatigue as they strain to listen to what is said, and generally leaves them with an unfavourable impression about teleconferencing.

- Video signals should be at a standard where sharply defined pictures with natural flesh tones are received. Broadcast quality pictures are not absolutely necessary for making a video telecon-ference a success.

- The video camera and receiving monitor should be positioned so as to maximize the illusion of eye contact. We found that placing the local (or transmitting monitor) below the receiving monitor, and keeping it relatively smaller, was less distracting and better for eye contact — people tend to look at themselves more (thus reducing the illusion of eye contact) if their own image is as prominent and as visible as that of the party at the far location.

- Graphic support aids should be integrated suitably into the sys-tem. These should work as they normally do in a face-to-face meeting environment. New techniques for presenting graphics tend to fluster users.

In short, the overall system should be as simple as can be to *adequately* and *reliably* do the job.

Teleconference Room Characteristics. The design of the room should differ as little from a typical meeting room as possible. If an organization typically has plush meeting rooms for the use of pro-fessionals, middle management, and executives, the teleconference rooms should match it in furnishings and general appearance. If, on the other hand, the rule is functional boardrooms, as in public service organizations, then teleconference facilities should be no different. Excessive lighting (especially flood lights), noisy air-conditioning, noise from adjacent areas or equipment rooms, poor ventilation, and smoke pollution all distract or dismay participants. Furniture should be designed for practical comfort, keeping in mind that teleconferences are more tiring than corresponding face-to-face meetings.

Accessibility. Our pilot project clearly established the need for a teleconference facility that was easily accessible to a majority of users. Under extreme weather conditions, people are especially reluctant to leave the office building to get to a teleconference facility located in a nearby place. For maximum utilization, users should be able to access the teleconference facility without leaving their office premises.

Experience has also shown that for effective utilization by a broad spectrum of organizational personnel, the teleconference facility should be located in a general meeting room area (for example, not next door to the executive office suites). If senior executives are committed teleconference users, a smaller, user-operated facility may be installed for their use in the executive wing.

User Awareness. User awareness programs regarding the concept of teleconferencing, its benefits, its applications; and when, how, and where it may be used, are essential for the success of teleconferencing. The awareness program must, of course, be designed to suit the organization. In this regard, introduction and success of teleconferencing is no different from that of any other new product or service — there is a direct payoff from proper promotional efforts.

It must always be emphasized during a promotional campaign and in all promotional material that teleconferences are not designed to replace all travel. People can be hostile towards a service that is perceived as a threat to their annual trips to conferences. All efforts must be made to generate an understanding that teleconferencing is yet another business tool — a management productivity aid — to be used at the discretion of the individual.

User Training. The first contact with teleconferencing is an important one for a new user. If an adequate description of the method of operation of the system is provided in *simple language,* and a knowledgeable person, a facilitator, is available to address questions or concerns that might arise during the session, the individual usually comes away with a positive feeling about teleconferencing. If this is followed by appropriate training or suggestions about the use of teleconferencing and the associated hardware (for applications relevant to the specific users), then continued use of the system can be expected.

The importance of appropriate user training cannot be over-emphasized. As a corollary to that, teleconference planners and system administrators must be genuinely receptive to the critiques and suggestions offered by users.

Teleconference Service Characteristics

Much has been said above about the desirable ergonomic characteristics of teleconference systems. However, it will be the overall service that will influence the acceptance of teleconferencing within an organization.

Service availability and reliability are the two important criteria in teleconferencing. For availability, the following should be considered:

- Who has access to the service?
- How is access gained; that is, what are the teleconference booking procedures?
- What is the lead time required for gaining access?
- Can promotional information be readily obtained?
- How frequently are service demonstrations held?
- What are the cancellation procedures and penalties, if any?
- What, if applicable, are the preemption criteria? (For example, if a vice president requires the use of the system on a demand basis, will his or her needs be met at the expense of another?) or will the use of the service be strictly on a first come, first served basis?)

Reliability of the service will depend upon the reliability of the weakest component of the system. This vulnerability could be in the hardware, or the result of an absenteeism problem on the part of a teleconference operator/facilitator. In all cases, at least one standby should be planned for each contingency. For example, telephones should always be available in the event a video teleconference system failure occurs. The users should be made aware of expected problems and reliability limitations.

Technical Considerations. Two types of technical considerations are examined below. The first follows from the human engineering and application requirements of the system, as detailed earlier. The second type deals with other technical factors resulting from currently available technology, cost/performance characteristics of hardware and other materials, and availability of transmission services; the latter are heavily dependent on the prevailing regulatory environment.

For purposes of discussion, the teleconference system will be divided into three building blocks:

• The teleconference room(s);

• The teleconference hardware; and

• The teleconference transmission medium.

Each of the building blocks will be further analyzed for audio and video requirements. See Figure 2-2 for a conceptual schematic.

The Teleconference Room. Information gathered from applications research and from human engineering considerations would indicate whether there should be rooms dedicated to teleconference services or shared with other meetings. The maximum number of people expected to participate in a teleconference will determine the room size.

Audio Requirements. Whatever the size of the room, its geometry should be considered at the time of selection or design of a room for use in teleconferencing. For example, long, narrow rooms tend to give the audio a reverberation effect.

The room should have good sound insulation — either built into the walls and ceiling or installed externally as acoustic wall panels and ceiling tiles. Carpeting on the floor is essential for further suppression of unwanted sounds. The exact nature of materials used for acoustic treatment would depend upon:

• Current status of room;

• Availability of materials; and

• Preferences of interior designers working for the organization.

Video Requirements. The walls and carpet in a teleconference room should not be dark in colour, as they absorb ambient light and produce a dark picture on the monitor. For a colour teleconference

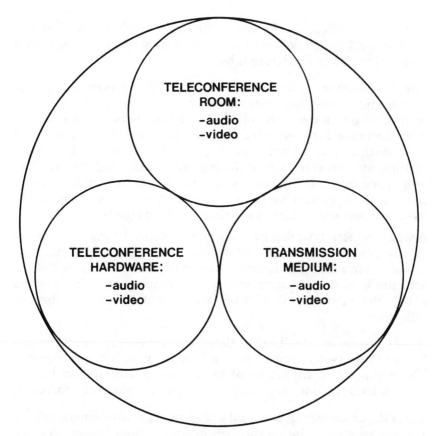

Fig. 2-2 Components of a teleconference system.

system, as well as for maintenance considerations, white walls or carpeting is not desirable. Neutral, pastel colours work best.

Since use of flood lights is not recommended for a teleconference room, it is essential that warm, daylight-type bulbs are used to maximize the illumination of the room at about a 3000 degree (Kelvin) colour temperature. A minimum of 125 foot candles (a measure of illumination) of uniform lighting is required for the type of cameras used in the current Ministry of Government Services system. The lights should be arranged in banks that can be switched individually so that during slide presentations, for example, selected areas of the teleconference room can be darkened.

Chrome finish on furniture is not practical for these rooms since light can be reflected off some of the surfaces. This contributes to distracting bright spots on the monitor as well as damage, over time, to the camera's picture tube.

The Teleconference Hardware for Single Camera Systems. Once it is determined whether multi-camera, remotely controlled systems, or single-camera user-controlled systems are required, a selection must be made between fixed *versus* transportable equipment. A room dedicated to teleconferencing calls for a fixed multi-camera installation, recessed in the walls and ceiling mounted, *et cetera.* For user-operated single camera systems, the decision to select a fixed or transportable system could hinge on whether one system will be used from several locations within a building complex.

A single camera system is suitable for user control. Small groups of 3 or 4 people are accommodated well with this set-up. Simultaneous use of human and graphic visuals is not practical. Figure 2-3 is a schematic of the arrangement of the components. The housing should be made of wood with an appropriate finish for low reflection.

Audio Requirements. Two to three low impedance microphones, featuring press-to-talk bars with a lock-down option, are required. The audio mixer should be of high quality, and should have a built-in 1000 Hz tone tone oscillator for system checking purposes.

Video Requirements. A three-tube camera capable of functioning in 125 foot candles of illumination without perceptible image retention would be required. The camera need not be top-of-the-line, broadcast quality. Investment in a low priced three tube camera and a high quality video receive monitor offers a good cost/performance trade-off. A 27-inch receive monitor is well liked by users. The transmit preview monitor for the participants need not be as high in quality and should be no larger that 17 inches, so that it does not draw attention away from the picture on the receiving monitor. Camera lens size and zoom ratios depend very much on room size and applications.

Teleconference Hardware for Multiple Camera Systems

The multiple camera system is remotely controlled from a control room which is ideally placed adjacent to the teleconference room so that the operator/technician can also serve as the facilitator.

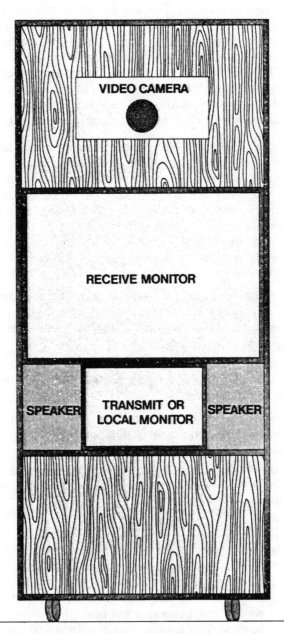

Fig. 2-3 Single Camera Teleconference System.

Audio Requirements. The applications will determine how many microphones should be made available. "Daisy chaining" low impedance microphones is most practical. Providing one microphone with a lock-down push-to-talk bar serves to add control to the meeting. This microphone should be set up for the chairman or main presenter in the meeting. Lapel microphones help make chalkboard or pad board presentations successful from the teleconference service point of view. The audio mixer is located in the control room.

Video Requirements. Applications, room availability, financial resource availability, and user preference influence the number of cameras to be used. While more cameras can be added at relatively little expense, video mixing and switching equipment become increasingly complex and costly. Most of the colour video switching equipment on the market today is designed for broadcast applications and must be purchased with many more features than are absolutely necessary. Small, simple video switches are currently available for two cameras and a key input.

In a two-camera system, if applications require the pick-up of much visual support material, one camera is best made mobile on a tripod. This way the camera can be moved to support visuals or to do "people shots."

In systems with more that two cameras, one camera can be dedicated solely to graphics. Again, lens sizes and zoom capabilities will depend on room size.

Numbers of receiving/transmitting preview monitors, with sizes as described for the one camera system, would depend again on room and audience size.

All video switching and mixing would be done in the control room with the aid of preview monitors on both the transmiting and receiving sides.

The Transmission Medium

Two levels of transmission facilities will complete the full-motion video teleconference link. From the teleconference room, the signals must get to the point of emanation of long distance transmission and, at the far end, signals must be received and fed into the teleconference room. This process must take place in both directions for a teleconference. Application requirements will govern whether both audio and video signals must flow in both directions or video in one direction only.

The local transmission facility for a system utilizing satellite communications may only be a cable run to the earth station on the roof of the building. For land-line or microwave long haul transmissions, a cable or local microwave system would be required to access the services of a common carrier.

Audio Requirements. Four-wire audio is usually available with both satellite and land-line links. Echos are more of a problem on satellite links, however. A variety of frequency shifters, echo suppressors, and cancelers are available on the market to help alleviate some of these problems.

A completely independent audio link for contingency use is absolutely necessary and vital to the continued success of a teleconference facility. This link can also be utilized to carry the audio of a video teleconference separately from the video signals, to provide minimum security.

If the telephone network is utilized for stand-by audio (its high reliability makes it a good choice) and if the video signals travel by satellite, visible loss of lip synchronization may result.

Security requirements on audio paths can be suitably met through selection of a scrambling/descrambling system from a wide range available on the market.

In some organizations (such as the Government of Ontario), the contingent audio link is used for continuing teleconferences on audio only, after doing a full-motion audio/video segment at the outset. This is done to limit costs.

Video Requirements. For true full-motion video teleconferencing, complete with eye contact and all non-verbal cues, a full TV channel (91 Mbps, or million bits per second) is required. Recent experimentation in video compression techniques has proved to be promising. It remains to be seen, however, if overall system performance can be maintained only by the use of top quality video equipment in the teleconference rooms.

For one-way video, two-way audio applications, satellite communication links are particularly suitable. The telephone network can be utilized for audio return from all the locations. Using this method, a large number of locations have been successfully linked for teleconferences.

For multi-location applications requiring two-way video and two-way audio, the set-up becomes more complex. For each location to view and hear everyone else, sophisticated switching and networking is required. Large numbers of video monitors are required in each teleconference facility, so that feeds from each location can be viewed. Speakers in each location would have to identify themselves when they spoke to avoid any confusion. The last two requirements would render the system formidable to the participant. System costs would also go up dramatically; not only because more hardware would be required, but also because more complex equipment would be required for service delivery. Moreover, greater expertise, both on the part of system operators, and on the part of users, would be needed. This would be expensive in terms of time and funds required for training.

Several audio/video scramblers are available on the market. These vary greatly in degree of security offered, price, and reliability of equipment. We thought that minimal scrambling (e.g., inversion on the video and well scrambled audio) using a commercially available device could result in well secured teleconference service. Individual system designers should survey the market for scrambling devices to meet their specific needs and budgets. With the advent of end-to-end digital networking for video teleconferencing, signal encryption for security should become readily available at an affordable price.

Administrative Considerations. The administrative component is vital to the proper functioning of teleconference service. Booking procedures, cancellation and preemption policies and practices, must be clearly formulated and strictly adhered to. A central and easily accessible (at least by telephone) point for booking must be designated and properly publicized.

Maintenance of daily system performance logs, user suggestion logs, and new and application files requires care and skill. It is not unusual for slippage to occur in the documentation of these parameters. Figure 2-4 is a randomly selected sample from the system log book maintained at our Thunder Bay teleconference centre.

An organization may choose to study travel expenses in order to introduce teleconferencing. This is an excellent method to zero in on potential dollar savings realizable through the use of teleconferencing. The study is best treated as a separate project, requiring detailed attention. A year's travel records can be analyzed for patterns, frequency, and reasons for travel. This information can be used to determine the initial locations and design of teleconference centres. The expenditure for travel can be used as a guide to potential savings. Once teleconferencing has been implemented, users

EXHIBIT 1

May, 25,/82
Teaching Seminar from 9-11 A.M.
2 people in T.O., 12 people in T.B.
Audio and video O.K.

June 1st/82
Doctor-patient interview, 9-10:30.
14 people in T.B., 1 in T.O.
Audio and video O.K.
Audio conference for Northern Affairs
Starting at approx. 1:05, 3 point
conference between T.B. Ottawa + Guelph.
4 people in T.B. over at 3:00.
Everyone was very pleased with
the audio conference system, the
meeting went according to schedule.

June 8/82
Demo for 4 members of Ontairo
Legislature from 10-10:30 - video
+ audio O.K. they seemed impressed.

Prepared by

Miss Irene Hietikko, Teleconference Operator
Thunder Bay Teleconference Centre

Fig. 2-4

will be asked to fill out a questionnaire (see sample, Figure 2-5) indicating whether they would have traveled as an alternative. Responses to these questionnaires can be used as a management tool for determining dollar savings, allocation of travel budgets for teleconferencing costs as well as level of user satisfaction. Getting users to fill out forms can be difficult. It is this administrative aspect of the project that needs the most careful attention and tact. Individual corporate needs would dictate how long this activity will continue.

Teleconference promotion staff, product support personnel, and maintenance personnel all need to be appointed and managed. System set-up procedures must be worked out clearly with all parties that contribute to the successful completion of a teleconference, such as common carriers.

Resource Requirements

Financial Resources. Other than capital costs which will depend

EXHIBIT 2

Complete after each teleconference and return to Coordinator.

TELECONFERENCING DATA SHEET

Name and Office/Division/Position ⎯⎯⎯⎯⎯   Date: ⎯⎯⎯⎯⎯⎯⎯⎯⎯⎯⎯

⎯⎯⎯⎯⎯⎯⎯⎯⎯⎯⎯⎯⎯⎯⎯⎯⎯⎯⎯⎯

Purpose of the Meeting ⎯⎯⎯⎯⎯⎯⎯⎯   Time:

⎯⎯⎯⎯⎯⎯⎯⎯⎯⎯⎯⎯⎯⎯⎯⎯   From: To:

System used (if choice is available): ⎯⎯⎯⎯⎯   ⎯⎯⎯⎯⎯   ⎯⎯⎯⎯⎯

⎯⎯⎯⎯⎯⎯⎯⎯⎯⎯⎯⎯⎯⎯⎯⎯⎯⎯⎯⎯

Participants

Location	Name and/or Number present	Travel?*	Hours	Savings $

Level of Satisfaction

1	2	3	4	5
Very Dissatisfied				Very Satisfied

*Indicate which parties would have travelled if no teleconferencing had been available.

Form developed for both audio and video teleconferencing by the TEMP Teleconferencing Task Force.

Fig. 2-5

heavily upon video and audio requirements, operating costs for use of network transmission facilities will be usage sensitive unless private lines are required. Operating expenses for technicians, facilitators, operators, and administrative personnel will depend upon the size and configuration of the system.

Human Resources. From the foregoing, it is clear that skilled people will be required to train users and promote, operate, maintain, and manage a teleconference service. The nature and size of the system will influence the actual number of people required. Smaller, user-operated systems can do with minimal on-site support. Resource sharing with other departments, especially for sites with low usage, is another way of controlling costs and keeping employees gainfully occupied.

THE GOVERNMENT OF ONTARIO OPERATIONAL SYSTEM
System Description

At the time of writing, the Government of Ontario video teleconference service is available in seven locations on a regular basis (see Figure 2-6). Four of the seven locations have teleconference facilities owned and operated by the Telecommunications Services branch, Ministry of Government Services. Existing meeting rooms have been upgraded and wired up in two of these locations to accomodate teleconferences as well as regular meetings. Teleconference equipment is wheeled in, set up before a teleconference, and removed afterwards. In a third location, an existing room was modified and used for teleconferencing only. In Oshawa, where a new Ontario government building was under construction, a new room was built specifically for teleconferencing. Bell Canada owns and operates the teleconference facilities in the other three locations and makes them available to its clients (such as the Government of Ontario), for a fixed fee per use. All local and long distance transmission links are also provided by Bell Canada.

In 1980, the Government of Ontario set up a multi-ministry task force to promote the concept of teleconferencing as an alternative to fuel-consuming travel throughout the government and the private sector. Pamphlets, brochures, audio-visual shows, demonstrations and personal interviews were used for promoting the concept and benefits of teleconferencing. Participation in trade and government shows also helped spread the message.

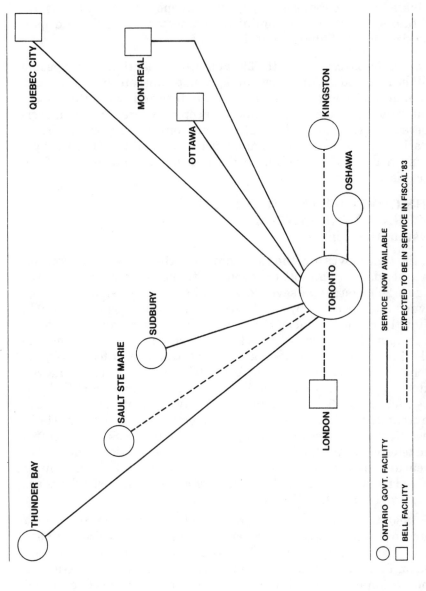

Fig. 2-6 The Government of Ontario operational system.

Applications and Human Factors. Initial applications for the first link of the network (Toronto-Thunder Bay) included regular administrative meetings, typically with overhead projector and pad board requirements. Most participants were middle managers and professionals communicating between head and regional offices. The use of visual aids was simplified through the use of two cameras. The meetings are made more comfortable for the participants by having technician-controlled equipment. The technicians at each end also facilitate the start of the meeting by explaining how to use the push-to-talk microphones, and the significance of the receive and local (or transmiting) signal monitors.

A first major application was in the area of health care delivery. Psychiatrists in Toronto provided consultations on difficult cases to attending physicians from the provincial mental health facility in Thunder Bay. This application called for a high degree of sensitivity to the patient's needs, removal of all system control to a technician's control room, confidentiality of all information exchanged, and a camera and monitor arrangement to provide close eye contact between doctor and patient as well as the transmission of non-verbal cues.

A remote seminar series was another "telehealth" application. With slide presentations and other visual aids, specialists in Toronto lectured to doctors and other medical staff from Thunder Bay. This called for a lecture room set-up with chairs arranged in theatre style in Thunder Bay, with the "lecturn" in Toronto. A lapel microphone was made available for the specialists and a "roving" microphone was used to gather questions from the seminar attendees. This set-up eased the free flow of questions since no one had to rise and walk to a microphone.

Seminar and training sessions in areas other than health care, such as affirmative action, retirement benefits, and the successful use of teleconferencing, are also taking place with increasing frequency.

Some interviews for personnel selection have also been conducted successfully using the video teleconference service. This use of teleconferencing had not been foreseen during the planning stages.

As the concept of teleconferencing and its benefits received wider acceptance, a new use for teleconferencing emerged. Members of the Ontario Legislature who, because of their tight schedules, could not arrange to travel to an important event or press conference, looked to teleconferencing as a solution. Special event teleconferences tend

to be closer to television productions, unlike regular business teleconferences. We find that using some studio lighting, skeleton script
preparation, and "stage direction" enhances the presentation of
such meetings.

Typically for executive use, the Government of Ontario also has
single-camera, user-controlled units installed in some offices. Several members of executive office staff are trained to set-up and use
these systems. All controls are housed in a low profile desk-top
control box, and complete instructions are put on the box on a plastic
card (see Figure 2-7). The single-camera user-controlled units plug
into the existing teleconference network. These units are also available for on-site use for the special event teleconferences just described. For large gatherings, the incoming video at the event site is
distributed to several video monitors or a large screen system strategically placed for the convenience of the audience. The incoming
audio is fed into the local public address system.

A cyclical trend in the use of teleconferencing as a substitute for
travel has also emerged over time. Usage falls significantly in
summer, when weather is more conducive to travel.

Technical Considerations. As described above, application requirements called for both two and one camera systems. In Ontario,
at this time, two-way local transmission links, as well as long haul
links, must be obtained from the common carriers. Of the two national carriers that serve Ontario (CNCP Telecommunications and
Telecom Canada/Bell Canada), only Bell Canada offers tariffed
video teleconference facilities and services at this time. Hence, all
transmission links in Figure 2-6 are provided by Bell Canada, at
monthly and usage sensitive rates. For the long distance charges,
the rating philosophy that is currently used by Bell Canada is that
one hour of video teleconference time should cost roughly as much
as one person's round trip airfare between the two locations under
consideration.

In keeping with the non-broadcast, but acceptable, signal quality
requirements stated earlier, equipment was selected for best cost/
performance ratio, good performance of the camera under low lighting levels and the availability of adequate servicing facilities in the
more northern locations. Figure 2-8 provides a list of equipment
typically in use. It must be noted this is not a product endorsement
for any manufacturer, but just a list of reliable equipment with
acceptable performance and price. It works well in our environment.

INSTRUCTIONS

1. Check that the lens cap is removed from the camera, and that the two TV monitors (television sets) are on. Also check that the microphone is connected into the front of the cabinet (to plug labelled MIC.2).

2. If the two TV monitors are not on, follow the instructions on the inside of the door at the rear of the cabinet.

3. Switch the ON/OFF POWER switch, on the remote control panel, to the ON position. The red light will indicate that the power is on.

4. Push the IRIS control to the up position: a picture will appear on the small monitor. Release the control when maximum brightness has been obtained.

5. Move the PAN AND TILT control left and right, up and down, to check the movement of the camera.

6. Turn the VOLUME control to the half way position. The hiss from the speakers will increase.

7. Depress the orange button and speak through the microphone. You will hear your voice through the speakers. This step just checks that your audio is being transmitted.

8. Re-check that all controls are working. You are now ready to start your teleconference.

9. After the teleconference is finished, please push down on the IRIS control until the picture on the small monitor disappears.

10. Instructions for disconnecting and storing equipment are on the inside of the door at the rear of the cabinet.

Fig. 2-7 Instructions for single camera, user-controlled units.

EXHIBIT 3

Equipment used for a Single-Camera Teleconference System

1   JVC KY-1900, 3 tube saticon colour camera with power supply

1   Cannon J10X10R 10:1 zoom

or

1   Cannon JX12R6:1 zoom

1   Vicon V3000PT pan and tilt unit for 24 VAC operation

1   Sony KX250/27" colour monitor with speakers (receive monitor)

1   Panasonic CT-110 MC 10" colour monitor (transmit or local monitor)

1   Shure M67 microphone mixer

1   AKG-D190E micorphone mounted on a Shure model 540A desk stand with push switch and AD-7B mic adapter.

1   Portable console of wooden construction to house above equipment

1   Vicon V113APT joystick controller

1   Canon CC-21T control

1   Desk top control unit housing all user controls

*Note: Specific room size and applications must be taken into consideration for zoom ratio selection: For example, a 10:1 zoom lens would not be required in a room 10' x 12' in floor area.

Fig. 2-8 Single camera video teleconferencing equipment list.

New equipment and other vendors are frequently evaluated to find something better for the same price, or less.

A few experimental items deserve mention. The newly constructed facility in Oshawa has three cameras — two for "people shots" and one for ceiling-mounted for visual aids. This configuration is under evaluation for performance and ease of operation.

A completely wireless version of the desktop box with a single camera system (see photograph, Figure 2-9) has also been developed for us by a manufacturer in Toronto. It uses infrared technology. This will replace all unsightly wires running between the single camera equipment and the teleconference table in the executive suite.

Ordinary meeting room tables and chairs (in lighter wood finish, without chrome) are used in all the Ontario government teleconference locations except Oshawa. A table in the shape of an elongated "C", with suitable outlets for microphone and cable placement, was custom built for Oshawa. This table is also under evaluation for practicality, user comfort, and effectiveness for close-ups of people and group camera work. Again, regular meeting room chairs are used.

Administrative Considerations and Resource Requirements. All teleconference booking is done through the teleconference unit at the Telecommunications Services Branch in Toronto. A minimum of forty-eight hours notice (working days only) is required by Bell Canada in order for their tariffed rates to apply. All bookings are confirmed with Bell Canada by TWX. Booking of common service meeting rooms is also done by the teleconference unit at Telecommunications Services Branch.

A full-time technician, who also serves as a teleconference operator and facilitator, is resident in Toronto. Assistant technicians and/or work term students are employed at other centres. In Sudbury, operational support is provided by people who look upon teleconferencing as a job enrichment opportunity.

A daily system performance log is maintained in all locations staffed by full-time personnel. The technician in Toronto has overall responsibility for trouble-free running of the system, for maintaining a general trouble log for all locations, and for following established escalation procedures for trouble clearance. He also coordinates successful turn-on and set-up of the service for each use. He is also responsible for proper service shut-down.

Until recently, most of the promotion was done through the Transportation/Energy Management Program Task Force on teleconferencing mentioned earlier. The Telecommunication Services Branch is taking over gradually the promotional activity as the task force winds down its role.

Training on the single-camera, user-controlled systems is provided by the teleconference staff members present at the location. These people receive their training from the Telecommunication Services Branch.

Fig. 2-9 Custom-built wireless microphone uses infrared technology to improve aesthetics of the meeting room.

Related Projects

This chapter has focused on video teleconferencing; however, video teleconferencing is only part of the teleconference services used in the Ontario government. The Ministry of Government Services also operates a government-owned audio teleconference bridge. This is used in conjunction with the public switched network and the government Inter-City Network of tie lines and foreign exchange lines to provide multi-location audio teleconferencing. This service supplements the video teleconference service in the following ways:

- It makes teleconferencing available wherever there is a telephone, affording greater flexibility in areas where it would be impractical to offer video teleconferencing.

- It provides multi-location teleconferencing; two-way video teleconferencing is presently available between only two locations at a time.

- It provides multi-location, two-way audio hook-up with a two-location video teleconference.

- It helps keep the cost of teleconferencing down — several users start their meeting with video teleconferencing to get that "real, in-person" feeling, and then continue with audio only.

It has been our experience that teleconferencing is promoted most effectively as an overall concept, with the specific application (and location) dictating which type of system, among those available, should be utilized. An audio teleconference network should be considered, wherever feasible, to supplement video teleconferencing.

Future Directions

In keeping with the idea of providing a range of services under the teleconference umbrella, the Ministry of Government Services is also examining some computer-based services. From the simultaneous, or real-time, teleconference point-of-view, Telidon technology is under consideration for teleconference visual aid support. Computer-based text and voice mail are already being used in a limited way to provide non-simultaneous or asynchronous teleconferencing. It is projected that use of computer-based store-and-forward messaging, both text and voice, will grow considerably over the next five years along with the use of video teleconferencing. The teleconference network will be expanded according to usage patterns and user needs.

THE AUTHOR

Neeru M. Biswas, P.Eng., has been Supervisor, Systems Development at the Telecommunication Services Branch of the Ontario Ministry of Government Services since September 1978. She has been responsible for the development, design, implementation, expansion, and maintenance of the Government of Ontario teleconferencing networks and systems — both audio and full-motion video. In that capacity, she served as coordinator for the Government of Ontario's participation in the Anik-B satellite program sponsored by the Canadian Department of Communications.

Mrs. Biswas has also been a member of the government's Transportation Energy Management Program Teleconferencing Task Force since its inception in early 1980. Currently, she is also responsible for the implementation and promotion of computer-based voice mail and integrated voice and data terminals within the Government of Ontario.

Previously, Mrs. Biswas worked as a Senior Systems Engineer with the Computer Communications Group of Bell Canada. As in her current position, she worked with users of telecommunication services, designing and developing systems technically and ergonomically tailored to their specific needs. Her earlier work experience was in Boston, Massachusetts, where she worked as Product Engineer at Unitrode Corporation.

Mrs. Biswas holds an Sc.M. degree (1973) in electrical engineering from Brown University, Providence, Rhode Island, and a bachelor's degree from Indian Institute of Technology, Kanpur, India. She has made several presentations on teleconferencing at both national and international conferences, and has authored articles (some jointly) on the same subject in professional publications.

LIFE & CASUALTY

LIFE & CASUALTY

LIFE & CASUALTY

LIFE & CASUALTY

Mr. Jackson and Ms. Cox raise some new issues in this chapter as they explain Aetna's motivation for establishing a cross-town video tele-conferencing link. They follow the progress of the implementation as it blossoms from a single link to a cross-country network. Significant productivity gains are discussed.

Chapter 3
Video Teleconferencing: Getting Better Mileage
Out of Meetings at Aetna Life & Casualty
Richard H. Jackson III and Diane Cox

On March 2 of 1982, Aetna Life & Casualty marked a significant anniversary — its Hartford to Windsor, Connecticut video teleconferencing system had been in full operation for one year. For those of us who had been with the project from the start — nearly a year of planning and construction preceded its first year of operation — it was an occasion, not just for celebration, but for reflection on what we had learned about this new and exciting system of communications.

Significantly, one of the most important conclusions to be drawn is that the benefits of video teleconferencing may not be confined to giant corporations such as Aetna, but may offer a number of opportunities for middle-sized or small companies with plants or offices in more than one location. These are companies which may have dismissed video teleconferencing as being feasible only for the *Fortune* 500 with offices across the country and throughout the world. For large or small companies, however, video teleconferencing can save money, not just by eliminating time lost in travel, but through shorter, better disciplined meetings which lead to quicker and better decision making and to increased productivity.

LOCAL VIDEO TELECONFERENCING
PAYS FOR ITSELF

Although Aetna is a part of the Satellite Business Systems network which supports video teleconferencing nationwide, it is the local, intra-company use of video teleconferencing that is described here. Video teleconferencing, as it is currently used at Aetna, spans not thousands of miles but just 9 miles — the distance between Aetna's main office in Hartford, Connecticut and the site of the Casualty Administration department in nearby Windsor. Nine miles may not seem a big separation, but Aetna's surveys taken prior to the use of video teleconferencing showed that meeting participants could spend as much as 1½ hours in round trips between the two locations.

The original application chosen for the video teleconference evaluation was meetings between the data processing department in the casualty division and the user groups it serves. The Casualty Data Processing Department was in the process of relocating to Windsor. A supervisor in the Systems Department was properly concerned about having the systems analysts move 9 miles from the users they served. The interaction between the two groups required approximately 2,000 people per month to meet from the two sites. When we estimated how much time would be used in transit, we decided this was an excellent application for video teleconferencing .

ASSESSING CURRENT AND FUTURE MEETING COSTS

The all-important first step any company must take before committing itself to video teleconferencing is a thorough survey of how many travel and work hours may be saved and what that adds up to in travel dollars. For Aetna, video's advantages were plain, since the company plans to further decentralize its offices. In dollars and cents, it came down to this: the cost of building a video teleconferencing system including construction of four video teleconferencing rooms, purchase of technical equipment, furnishings, and installation came to $950,000. While Aetna had *projected* it would save this in lost time over a seven-year period, *actual* use has reduced that recovery time to four years.

Strict cost accounting and extensive research are part of "doing it right the first time." A company must determine its needs not just for the present but for the future. Assuming that a video teleconferencing system eventually will need to be expanded, it is practical to make the full commitment in planning and money at the beginning rather than to adopt a simplified system, which may have to be scrapped and replaced or updated at much greater expense in the future.

FULL-MOTION
VIDEO TELECONFERENCING SELECTED

After Aetna made the basic commitment to video teleconferencing, it had to determine what kind of system to use. There are several ways a company can go. The simplest and least expensive is audio teleconferencing which seems to work best in a situation in which visual interaction is not necessary. A stop-action video teleconference system, in which a series of still pictures is transmitted, is more expensive than audio teleconferencing, but allows for objects like flow diagrams and charts to be viewed at both sites without prior distribution. The last alternative Aetna considered was a full-motion video teleconference system.

An Aetna task force was appointed to consider all the alternatives. The task force made the decision to use full-motion video with two conference rooms in Hartford and two in Windsor.

MATRIX ORGANIZATION ADOPTED
FOR PROJECT MANAGEMENT

We used a matrix organization in the task force to coordinate the multiple facets required. The members of the task force were drawn from Corporate Communications, Corporate Data Processing, the casualty group's data processing department, the Facilities Management Department, the local telephone company, and an architect. The Corporate Communications Department (or more simply stated, the Television Operations Unit) provided the equipment and room design while Corporate Data Processing was responsible for the communications links between the two sites. The advantages of such a division of responsibility paid off. For example, the television people have experience with the human factors in communications systems, are aware of how video can be used to the maximum effect, and can work closely with those who will use the system. While the Corporate Data Processing Department was also capable in human engineering matters, its telecommunications experience was valuable in structuring the best arrangement for the link-up.

COAXIAL CABLE USED FOR LOCAL LINK

Although satellites are often used for video teleconferencing over long distances, shorter links may successfully use microwave, light wave, or land lines. In Aetna's case, it was decided to use coaxial cable to connect the two locations. While Aetna's research showed that fiber optic cable might have been as effective as coaxial cable, the telephone company from which the lines are leased could not make fiber optics available in 1981.

ROOM DESIGN CONSIDERATIONS

When the time came to design the video meeting rooms, our overriding consideration was to create conditions under which the self-consciousness which results from being "on the air" would be minimized to enhance the flow of communications. With that in mind, we wanted the video teleconferencing rooms to be like regular meeting rooms and not like television studios. We were very precise about the design of the meeting table, the placement of microphones, the size and placement of monitors, and the kinds of visual aid facilities needed in formulating our room design.

We started by building a mock-up room to which we invited groups of potential meeting participants. We quizzed them extensively about their reactions to various arrangements of table, microphones and technical equipment. Our final design evolved from these interviews. We chose a V-shaped table so that all participants could see one another without needing to crane their necks.

Our research showed that roughly 80% of all meetings involved no more than three people at each site and the largest meeting was with six participants. Consequently, we designed the table with seating for six; however, as many as twenty can be seated if a row of chairs is added around the edge of the room. (See Figure 3-1).

A small control panel, no harder to operate than the controls of a television set, is placed near the apex of the "V" of the table. The panel allows one of the participants to control an overhead black-and-white camera used to capture images such as charts, printed pages or visuals.

We were concerned that voice-activated microphones would create awkward situations as unintended sound could capture the attention of the audio system. Instead, a flush-mounted microphone in front of each participant handles the audio pick-up in the least obtrusive way.

Meeting participants face a front wall containing three 25-inch color television monitors. The two monitors portray a split-image panorama of the people seated at the V-shaped table at the other site. The third monitor is blank except when used to display supplemental visual material which may be placed on the table or lightbox, on a dry marker board, or on a screen as slides. In keeping with the findings of the survey, no monitors are used to allow the participants to see themselves. Color cameras, concealed behind the front wall, are used to cover the participants.

Fig. 3-1 Aetna's video teleconferencing room illustrating V-shaped table and multiple monitors in comfortable surroundings.

In Hartford, we are fortunate to have the two meeting rooms adjacent to one another. This arrangement permits the two rooms to share a common control center in a space created between the two rooms. Equipment controllers and some test equipment would otherwise have been duplicated.

There is a Group II-III facsimile machine in the room for transmission of documents between the two locations. This simulates the normal procedure of "passing papers around" as is common in a face-to-face meeting. When used in Group III mode, the facsimile can transfer a page in less than a minute. For larger documents, the material should be distributed prior to the meeting.

The size of the television monitors was a major subject of our design research. We decided against using a large screen, as is often employed in video teleconferencing rooms, on the grounds that the participants would be overly self-conscious when seeing each other on "larger-than-life" monitors. The room size would also have needed to be larger and a single large screen would not have allowed the type of continuous presence we were attempting to maintain through the video medium.

ROOM SCHEDULING
CONTRIBUTES TO HIGHER PRODUCTIVITY

Scheduling meetings was another area in which basic decisions had to be made. How much time should be allotted for each meeting? We decided on 45 minutes because our testing showed that meetings booked for one hour rarely lasted longer than 45 minutes. Herein lies an advantage of video teleconferencing over face-to-face meetings: with a strict timetable, meetings run much more efficiently. In fact, many meetings run well under the 45 minute limit. We also have found that next-level supervisory personnel are more willing to sit in on a meeting if they know that they will not be trapped in a prolonged session. We found that decisions are more often made on the spot during a meeting when decision-makers are involved as participants in progress meetings. This process allows action to be taken more quickly than in the conventional "up-the-ladder" memo fashion. Thus, we have better and quicker decision making — both vital to greater productivity.

After we had our initial experience with the test groups, we learned that in many cases it was desirable to involve people in the meeting for less than the full duration. To accomodate this need, we installed an audio-conference system in each room to allow additional people to be "called into the conference" when the situation arose. This has worked out quite well and is appreciated by those who are spared involvement in long meetings.

BEHAVIORAL IMPACT
OF VIDEO TELECONFERENCING

What is the effect of video teleconferencing on the participants themselves? How do people accept the idea of being face-to-face, not with other people, but with their images? Despite the advantages of time and money saved, are there disadvantages in the way people react to the meeting? To learn the answers, Aetna conducted a post-use survey.

During the first week of operation, all employees were invited to tour the rooms and to participate in a training program. This program was promoted actively in the company newsletter and in the cafeteria. A copy of the three-fold reference card we use for training is shown at the end of this chapter. Although there was some initial uneasiness by some participants in early meeting experiences, almost all discomfort has dissipated. Those who have had some experience with the rooms are now comfortable with them. New users of the rooms are helped through their anxiety by veteran users who have had similar misgivings.

The greatest proof of the system's success is that the rooms are now reserved many days in advance, and usage has been heavy. For example, from March 1, 1981 through August 31, 1982, 35,956 people were involved in 5,985 meetings via video teleconferencing. There are peaks in the demand for the rooms from 9:00 a.m. to 11:30 a.m. and from 1:00 p.m. to 3:00 p.m. But people are willing to schedule their meetings at lunchtime if they cannot get one of the preferred periods.

Another decision we made was in the area of cost allocation. We decided, and we are glad we did, to absorb the cost of video teleconferencing as an overhead item within the divisions housing the meeting rooms. If, as we believed, video teleconferencing results in higher productivity, we were not willing to risk those gains by having each manager second-guess whether a meeting could be afforded. Since the expenses of the system were going to be in place whether they were used or not, the allocation process could have had the undesirable effect of discouraging use.

Another important decision to be made was on the matter of priority use. We decided that a policy which would preclude *bumping* based on organizational rank would be preferred. People were to be encouraged to use the rooms and to plan their time. The use of a bumping system would have discouraged people from taking the risk of having a meeting canceled because of someone else's unplanned needs.

EXPANSION PLANNED

By 1985, we plan to have eleven video teleconference rooms in operation in the Hartford area with connections to our offices in Windsor, Middletown, and to our national satellite network. Our first "national" location, Chicago, joined the network on-line via Satellite Business Systems satellite service in February 1983. (See Figure 3-2.)

A survey was mailed to 800 individuals to learn about meetings requiring travel between Hartford and Washington. Of the 375 responses, 36% indicated they would use video teleconferencing meeting rooms as a substitute for travel between those cities. From these results, we were able to estimate that we would need 100 meeting hours per month to satisfy this demand. This was equivalent to three units of satellite time, each unit committing us to 40 hours of use per month. Washington, D.C. joined the network on November 10, 1983.

CONCLUSIONS

On the national level, at least, it seems clear that video teleconferencing may revolutionize the ways in which people meet, communicate, and conduct business in the coming decade. Time and money saved in travel are the most obvious positive results. Marketing methods may change dramatically if dispersed sales personnel can meet daily. Hiring patterns may be affected if preliminary interviews can be done by video. Companies have held press conferences and annual meetings by satellite. The Public Broadcasting System has begun to get into the business by making its facilities available for video teleconferencing, and many hotel chains now offer video teleconferencing at sites around the country. Video teleconferencing is quickly becoming less of a curiosity and more of a business fact-of-life.

Aetna has made a commitment to this new world of communications through its partnership in Satellite Business Systems. As for

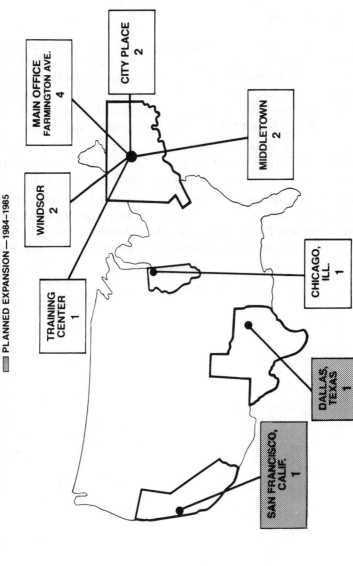

PLANNED ÆTNA TELECONFERENCING NETWORK IN 1983

PLANNED EXPANSION—1984–1985

TRAINING CENTER 1

WINDSOR 2

MAIN OFFICE FARMINGTON AVE. 4

CITY PLACE 2

MIDDLETOWN 2

CHICAGO, ILL. 1

DALLAS, TEXAS 1

SAN FRANCISCO, CALIF. 1

Fig. 3-2 Aetna's planned teleconferencing network as of 1983. Numerals at each location signify the number of active or planned meeting rooms.

local video teleconferencing, we have proven to our satisfaction that it pays dividends in time and money saved and in quicker decision making.

THE AUTHORS

Richard H. Jackson III is a Director in Corporate Communications for Aetna Life and Casualty, the nation's largest publicly held insurance and diversified financial services organization, with which he has been associated for more than 25 years. In his current capacity, he is responsible for the design and operation of all audio-visual facilities within Aetna's decentralized operation.

In 1983 Jackson was selected by *Telespan Newsletter* as the first recipient of its "Teleconferencing Professional of the Year" award. Telespan is a well respected teleconferencing publication.

He is past President of the Connecticut Valley Chapter of the Informational Film and Video Producers Association and a director of the International Teleconferencing Association. He is currently serving his fifth term as Selectman in his home town of Somers, Connecticut.

Diane Cox is a free-lance writer.

**Ætna
Teleconferencing
User
Guide**

Fig. 3-3

Preparation—Prepare for your teleconference as you do for face-to-face meetings. Use an agenda.

Entrance—Enter your scheduled room at the appointed time of your meeting. To ensure privacy, turn IN-USE light ON as you enter the room. Do not forget to turn the IN-USE light OFF as you leave.

Seating—Meeting leader should sit in front of the control panel (see opposite page).

Control Panel—Only necessary when you are going to use graphics. Take a moment to become familiar with it. First, press the GRAPHICS SWITCH to either LOCAL or REMOTE which enables you to view the graphics of the other room or your own. Next, if you want to view your graphics, press the button for the graphic medium you want. . . .

A. **Chalkless Board Controls**—The "joy stick", on the far left, moves the camera in all directions (pan and tilt). The adjacent rocker switch is for zoom control.

B. **Overhead Camera Controls**—The top right VIEWER button is to turn the back light on/off for transparencies. The left rocker switch is for the zoom control. The right knob is for focusing.

C. **Slide Controls**—Open the slide compartment door, on the right front wall, and load the carousel projector with your slide tray. Adjust the slide sequence with the black and white monitor. Close the door and return to the control panel. There are two buttons for forward and reverse.

D. **Still Send**—You MUST press this button each time you wish to send (transmit) your graphic (picture) to the other room.

Facsimile Machine—To send or receive printed documents, have patience. . . .once connected, it takes 30 seconds to transmit each page.

● make sure your machine is on

● tell the opposite room to make sure their machine is on

● to send-place document(s) face down in the sending tray; slide in until the READY light goes out

● ask the opposite room for the telephone number

● dial the number and listen for the tone; upon hearing the tone, depress the START button and hang up the receiver.

● to make copies-place document(s) face down in the sending tray; slide in until the READY light goes out; depress the COPY button.

Phone—For reservations or assistance please call (203)-273-0392.

A. **Conference Calls**—Use the phone in the front left of the room. Dial the desired party. Once connected, switch to CONFERENCE call and hang up the receiver. The persons voice will be carried by the room audio system to both rooms. When complete, switch back to NORMAL call.

B. **Emergency**—Should you lose audio, video or both you may continue your meeting while the problem(s) is being worked on. Use the phone in the front left wall. Call the conference phone in the other room. Once connected, depress the gold button on the upper right side of the phone set and hang up the receiver. When completed, press the on/off button. You can get the telephone numbers of any room by calling (203)-273-0392.

- use an agenda

- stick to the appropriate subject at hand

- effective control

- preparation

Use of the facilities may be arranged by contacting (203)-273-0392.

Development of audio-visual materials for use in the tele-conferencing rooms may be arranged by contacting the audio visual presentation office (203)-273-2299.

TIME IS VERY IMPORTANT!!! Remember . . . another teleconference may be scheduled immediately following your teleconference. Please leave on or before your scheduled time.

This facility is fully automated. You are not required to activate or shut off any systems.

A. Face the person(s) you are speaking to.

B. Speak naturally. Don't shout or whisper.

C. Do not touch cameras or TVs.

D. Have patience when using the facsimile.

E. Relax and enjoy your teleconference.

F. Call (203)-273-0392 if you need assistance.

EAR PLUG

There is an ear plug for anyone that has a hearing problem . . . located under the table at the right front seating position.

Fig. 3-4

GouldNet

Worldwide Telecommunications Networking

- Voice
- Data
- Electronic Mail
- Teleconferencing

Mr. Hart explains how a revolutionary change in the corporate strategy of Gould Inc. was the motivation for the establishment of their video teleconferencing network, Gouldnet. As Gould moved from industrial products to high-technology electronics, they found their product life cycles shrinking from decades to a few years. Video teleconferencing has enabled them to increase engineering productivity and hasten product development.

Chapter 4
The Development of Video Teleconferencing
at Gould Inc.
John R. Hart

It was apparent in 1979 that the information revolution was upon us before we were ready to use or adapt to it. At that time, Gould recognized the need to exploit the technology base and resources of telecommunications as a tool to improve productivity and profitability. Many problems needed to be identified and then solved along the way. The purpose of this chapter is to address the research, planning, and implementation for the slow-scan, or freeze-frame video teleconferencing network within Gould.

GOULD: THE COMPANY'S REDIRECTION

An introduction to teleconferencing at Gould begins with a short review of the company. In the late 1970s Gould, then a $2 billion company, was beginning one of the most dramatic changes that any American company had undergone in the last decade, changing its complexion from industrial products to electronics. The change was based upon management's decision to develop a business that could achieve the high profit margins produced by electronic products and to provide for further growth of the company. It was obvious that higher profits could be obtained through a redeployment of assets to electronics, and higher growth could be achieved in six of the highest growth markets in electronics.

The change toward this end which began in the late 1970s is near completion in 1984, and has created an "information revolution" within the company.

As an industrial company, our product life cycle was anywhere from twenty to thirty years, and the rapid need for information interchange did not play an important role in the productivity or profits of the company. However, as Gould began evolving into an electronics company, timely decisions became critical. Product life cycles in the electronics industry are more in the neighborhood of 18 to 36 months. Clearly, the company had to move information more rapidly, and make timely decisions based on that information. Gould's management understands that telecommunications is a means of helping resolve the demands created by this information revolution.

First, a high quality voice telecommunications network was developed and implemented. This network, "Gouldnet" (see attached network map, Figure 4-1), linked together the major locations throughout Gould, thus allowing availability of transmission services on a more timely basis for the voice communications.

Second, an electronic data network was designed, to be implemented in three segments. The first phase will involve the building of an electronic data network based on the X.25 technology, duplicating the same routes as the voice network. The data network will allow the same speed and ease of communications for the data operations that the voice network allows. The second phase of the plan includes the implementation of electronic mail systems and the integration

Gould Teleconferencing Network

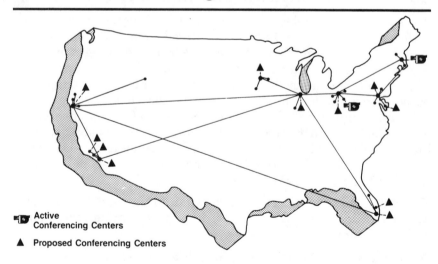

◼📷 Active
    Conferencing Centers

▲ Proposed Conferencing Centers

Fig. 4-1 Gouldnet telecommunications route map.

of dissimilar mail systems currently installed. Third, the plan incorporates a video teleconferencing network to complement the voice and data communications system.

Telecommunications within Gould is looked upon as a resource and not an expense. Gould fully supports and encourages technological advancement, the increased utilization and implementation of high technology telecommunications systems — thus, the development of Gouldnet, the telecommunications network for Gould.

TELECOMMUNICATIONS TECHNOLOGY FOR PRODUCTIVITY

Gould recognizes that overall employee productivity must be improved if the company is to compete in the electronic product market. Identifying productivity became a critical issue. If productivity in engineering, production, and marketing is not consistent with the time frame of the competitive marketplace, the company might miss a significant opportunity. The result would be either loss of market share or marginal gain in targeted markets.

Gould made the commitment for the transformation of their management processes to meet the challenges of the electronics industry. The company faced productivity improvement problems head on. A productivity improvement center (quality circles) was developed, emphasizing to all employees the importance of the mental attitude that must be in place to address the "electronic information age" within the company.

By setting up quality circles throughout the company, manufacturing productivity issues were addressed by both management and production employees. Office productivity was addressed through office automation, and the introduction of terminals on the manager's desk aided the rapid dissemination of information. The interface of manufacturing productivity, office automation, and systems integration has proved to be the key factor in solving the information crisis created by the shift from traditional to electronic products. Telecommunications plays an important role in these efforts by the implementation of voice and data networks, the interface of unlike computer systems, and through the introduction of slow-scan teleconferencing networks. The current video systems used are a combination of both high quality audio conferencing equipment and slow-scan compression hardware.

Telecommunications is looked upon as the leading force for the introduction of these technologies into the business environment. The capability necessary to tie all the information together is provided via the telecommunications networks. The channels of communications between engineers, research and development, production people, and management bring together the information needed to produce a product in a timely manner to compete in the fast-paced electronics industry.

VIDEO TELECONFERENCING IN A DECENTRALIZED COMPANY

The current makeup of Gould is that of an extremely decentralized company, coordinated by a minimal corporate overhead structure. Gould is divided into four operating units, each targeted at a specific marketplace: electronic products; electronic components; electronic systems; and research and defense systems. These four major units rely heavily on the need to communicate, and video teleconferencing helps support this need.

The first step taken by Gould's Telecommunications Department was to locate operations that would benefit from rapid communications. The areas which needed to be fully understood and reviewed were:

Areas To Be Reviewed

- **Production/Shop Floors**
- **Engineering Departments**
- **Product Development Centers**
- **Research and Development Labs**
- **Administrative Staffs**
- **Finance Departments**

Fig. 4-2 Areas targeted by Gould for video teleconferencing.

After a comprehensive analysis of their problems, they realized that the needs of all these user groups were the same. They needed information on a more timely basis. This would enable them to make better decisions, thus bringing the products to the market sooner, and strengthening the company's position in the industry.

A basic review of the problem-solving cycle to determine applications may be helpful at this point:

- Recognize that a problem exists
  - interview user departments and associated departments
  - management interviews at all levels
  - resolve the problem with the users
- Review the alternatives
  - hardware/software
  - vendor comparisons
  - review with the users
- Select the best answer
  - organize the alternatives
  - cost/benefit analysis
  - review with the users
- Sell the concept internally
  - users
  - management
- Implement the system
  - system training
  - project manager
- Review the findings
  - review costs and benefits
  - analyze the savings
  - further define the project's objectives

Identifying the individual needs of each user became part of selling the ideas back to the user. This internal selling cycle actually begins by working with the individual managers and pinpointing the problems with them. The major problem may be in quality control, it may be a production part mismatch, it may be the need for drawings or engineering changes in a more timely manner. Whatever the problem, the need to transmit information, both verbally and visually, is paramount to resolving the problem.

Problem-Solving Cycle

- **Recognize That a Problem Exists**
- **Review the Alternatives**
- **Select the Best Answer**
- **Sell the Concept Internally**
- **Implement the System**
- **Review the Findings**

Fig. 4-3 A summary of Gould's problem-solving cycle.

An outline summary of the process used in selling the idea is:

- Understand the company goals at all levels of the organization
  - read the plans of all the departments involved
  - understand the business segment the company is marketing
- Work with operational units and understand the business from their viewpoint
  - meet with the department heads and staff
  - understand their business and functional operations
- Help them understand their problems, review these problems with each manager
  - help them identify their own problems
  - encourage them to make the recommendation for solving these problem
- Begin selling the idea when the problem finding is occurring
  - have the user solve the problem
  - reinforce the users
- Each manager should be a part of the solution
  - system selection
  - system implementation
- Discuss, in the users terms, the problem and the solution, leaving out the technical jargon

Selling The Ideas

- **Understanding the Company Goals**
  - Read Departmental Plans
  - Understand Business
- **Work from the Users Viewpoint**
  - Meet with Departments
  - Understand their Operation
- **Help Users Understand Problem**
  - Help the Users Find the Problem
  - Let the Users Find the Resolution
- **Sell the Idea When the Problem is Found**
  - Have the Users Solve the Problem
  - Reinforce the Users' Decision
- **All Users Must Be a Part of Solution**
  - System Selection
  - System Implementation
- **Discuss the Problem and Solution in the Users' Terms NOT Technical Jargon**

Fig. 4-4 Gould's model of the internal selling process.

Selling the idea is an extremely easy proposition once the need of the users is identified by the user. (This is the key to the success of the program.) Having done that, one can implement the process by demonstrating the product and showing how the technology can be used to solve the problems. When users participate in the review of the equipment, they actually sell themselves on the resolution of the problem.

For example, if the users have the need to transmit a document from the East Coast to the West Coast in less than a minute, bring to their attention the attributes of a facsimile machine in conjunction with the video system. However, if the need is for face-to-face interaction, as would be required during engineering change orders, demonstrate how this can be handled more efficiently through video teleconferencing. Addressing problem solving through user participation overcomes the natural reluctance to trust the unknown.

Once this was accomplished at Gould, it was then easy for the Telecommunications Department to begin designing the systems, keeping in mind the needs and applications of each and every user. The involvement and constant interaction with the users, in both the problem recognition and the problem solving stages, made progress easier during the selling stage of the program.

System criteria and design were based on the interactive needs of the users. One alternative reviewed was full-motion video, including compression video at 1.544 Mbps (million bits per second). This alternative was discarded since only a small percentage of the actual meetings (less than 6%)* required a face-to-face encounter. Therefore full-motion video did not meet the needs for the majority of the meetings. Most of the meeting interface and interaction required only the transfer of information in the working environment (for example, discussions involving blueprints or component parts). Another application was the need to present a slide show during a meeting. For these purposes, slow-scan, or freeze-frame video teleconferencing was introduced and has become successful. These were the first applications addressed.

Promoting the interactive use of the system took some initial training. We had to overcome many of the problems which the users see as a negative for video conferencing in a slow-scan environment — for example, the transmission time to deliver the picture to the other location. The current equipment in use allows the transmission of a picture from point A to point B in approximately 30-38 seconds, depending on the density of the picture. With this option, the speeds can be increased or decreased, depending on the application.

In most cases, we found users began pacing their presentations, and their conversation, to fit the speed of the equipment. We also found the information being transmitted was better organized and more effective than in the past. As users became more comfortable with the equipment, they also become better organized in terms of time management, preparation, and presentation skills. Thus, we were

---

*Based on AT&T studies.

able to create a more productive worker, and one who takes pride in showing his information to his peers.

Slow-scan truly encompasses productivity improvement, resulting in enhanced skills for the person using the system. Users also began to have more meetings, and to disseminate more information. The meetings held with the system users were shorter than the face-to-face meetings in the past, resulting in net gains in both effective communications and time saving.

Physical system design is important for maximizing results. While design is based on the applications of each individual user, it is important to ensure compatibility between the systems that are individually developed throughout the company, keeping in mind the corporate focus for the program. A unit on the East Coast should be compatible with a unit on the West Coast. The main intent was to design a system so that if a need arises to transfer information across divisional lines, the equipment is available and compatible.

Standardization of transmitting and receiving equipment was one of the key areas of concern as the user base developed independently throughout the corporation. Because we were looking for systems that were compatible, we selected one vendor. The equipment had to be flexible, expandable, and of high quality and high resolution. We also looked for equipment that was mobile enough to be moved from location to location in a reasonably short time. In certain high-volume locations, particular attention must be paid to the environment in which the teleconferencing equipment is located.

The teleconferencing function, of course, was to support the communication needs of the specific users — engineering and production — and to help increase the productivity of their employees. The room was designed with excellent sound-proofing and acoustics, utilizing high grade audio systems. It was also designed for silent operation with the projection equipment built behind a glass wall. This multi-media room not only serves the function of teleconferencing, but also as a standard conference room.

As basic management practices have taught us in the past, the hardware is extremely important. Colorado Video equipment was selected based on high quality and cost performance. They provided the service required for system design and implementation. We also found complete compatibility within the product line. The Chicago-based distributor, Televideo Consultants, served as the agents for the test project. The distributor's assistance was invaluable for training, information, and coordination of the entire system.

Conceptual Conference Room

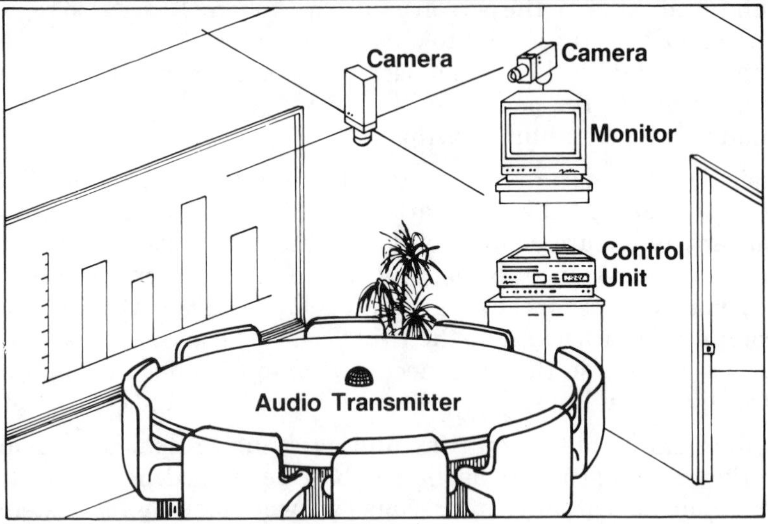

*Fig. 4-5 Gould's conference rooms are used for video and audio
teleconferencing and ordinary business meetings.*

The sound equipment used was the Darome convener unit with a
pressure-sensitive microphone mounted in the middle of the table.
This combination allowed for a high quality audio conference, with
or without the slow-scan video equipment from Colorado Video.
Thus, the rooms used in teleconferencing throughout Gould can
be independently used for high quality audio meetings. These audio
conferences represent a major segment of the meetings conducted in
these rooms. As mentioned above, the rooms are designed to be
multi-purpose. When video teleconferencing or audio conferencing
are not in session, the rooms can be used as standard meeting rooms,
for slide shows and multi-media shows — thus providing the company with the most cost effective approach to a conference room.
(See Fig. 4-5).

The basic concept for the room design comes from a variety of
different sources. Research studies have been conducted in the teleconferencing centers of other major companies throughout the United States. Gould has incorporated the findings and applications
from those companies into our conference centers. The integration
of ideas from other companies was also a part of the internal selling
cycle for Gould to sell the idea of teleconferencing to the users.

In designing the rooms, we called upon people from several internal departments — facility planners, audio engineers, administrative managers — and asked them to help identify how the perfect conference room should function. It was easier to sell the idea if the different disciplines in management were part of the decision making process from the very beginning. The same approach that was used in selling the idea of teleconferencing was also used in the implementation process. You really do not have to sell the person at that point. He is already part of the solution making; the sale is made easier.

For the future direction of video teleconferencing equipment, we are reviewing the interface to computer graphics. The approach in this area is to integrate an interactive graphics terminal to the slow-scan freeze-frame equipment. We expect this to be in operation by late 1984. The purpose for this direction is to assist in CAD/CAM (computer-aided design/computer-aided manufacturing), and computer-aided engineering applications in the engineering departments.

INTEGRATING THE SYSTEM
INTO THE WORKING ENVIRONMENT

As was mentioned earlier, the planning process and implementation of the system must be reinforced and supported by the users. It can never be repeated enough that the users must:

The Users Must

- ● **Identify Their Own Problem**
- ● **Solve Their Own Problem**
- ● **Be a Part of Decision-Making Process**

Fig. 4-6 The role of the user in problem solving.

The objectives for implementation were created by the needs of the users. Once the user identified these needs, he also helped set the objectives for the implementation of the system that would resolve the problems. Each user was identified ahead of time and became an integral part of the planning process, actually reviewing the systems in advance, and discovering how the different types of equipment would serve their needs.

A team approach to installation was the key to the success of the system. A system manager was assigned to each project location involved in the program. A person on the local level was responsible for the installation and implementation of all the systems. The team approach also ensured vendor participation aimed at on-time construction, installation, and training. Information packages were distributed to all users, trial runs were set up, and the conference room suppled with the appropriate aids — writing materials, clean blackboards, etc. The project manager also assured the presence of audio/visual personnel to support the needs of the meeting. These are the main responsibilities of the project manager, and will continue as part of the on-going program.

The importance of project management cannot be stressed enough, and is a key ingredient for success. You must find the person who is sufficiently interested in the project to support and sell it continuously to the potential users. A strong manager also has an emotional impact on the project. If the manager is enthusiastic and excited about what is happening with the technology which he is managing or implementing, that enthusiasm is extended to the users. The manager should stress that the system is there to help the organization grow and strive for goals that the entire company is seeking —increased productivity, increased profits, and growth.

An enthusiastic manager also helps overcome the emotional changes, or the "negative downside," that some managers have identified with teleconferencing. Many authors have written that teleconferencing is a negative approach to productivity. Basically, they are saying that the negative impact is overpowering the benefits and slowing the development of teleconferencing. However, if the emotional issues are identified and shared with the users, the project manager can overcome these conceptions. Some of the negative impact occurs when the non-mechanical problems are not addressed at the onset of the project. If properly discussed and planned these issues can be turned into advantages from the users' perspective.

It is often stated that slow-scan teleconferencing will displace travel. On the contrary, we address slow-scan not as a travel displacement issue, but as a complement to existing meeting schedules. For example, an engineer who needs to fly to the West Coast twice a month can still do so now, but in addition he can conduct two or three teleconferences. The engineer solves more problems through teleconferencing by increasing information flow, and discussing prob-

ard sell" the program. We still encourage program use, and we
ll solicit new users through peer group acceptance of the system.
w users are identified almost on a weekly basis. New teleconfer-
es are set up promptly and operated by the administrator. Man-
rs frequently request a teleconference on very short notice. "Can
a accommodate me?" This request for improved communications
ecoming more commonplace as the system becomes entrenched
o the way we conduct business.

s always important, though, to reinforce the marketing or the
ling of the idea. We use a multi-sided approach. The manager of
system, divisional management, department heads, and the
tem administrator are continually reinforcing their belief in the
tem. This reinforcement strengthens the overall selling and ac-
tance. Peer pressure and the discovery of the way the system
ves problems are other selling approaches. The external force of
nagement and the internal force of peer group acceptance to-
her sell the system.

W THE SYSTEM MEETS THE NEEDS
MANAGEMENT

with any other capital equipment purchase, these questions must
answered:

ow is the system's effectiveness to be measured?

ow is productivity to be measured?

e teleconferencing equipment is no different from a drill press, a
v lathe, a new production machine, or a new assembly line. It is
peting for the available capital dollars. Therefore, we have
nd a way to evaluate the process and measure its worth. The
owing chart is the result of the program we hope to achieve. If a
ject cycle can be reduced by 10% through increased meetings,
n teleconferencing will be considered successful. (See Figure 4-7.)

can assign a dollar value on the engineer's productivity im-
vement by placing a value on how much sooner a product is
ught to market with the aid of the system. This is done by the
rs. They tell us if the system is worth what they are paying for
ng it. Better decision making, by virtue of more information
ng available on a timely basis, is another method of cost-
tifying the system. Most companies wrestle with how to measure
s issue. It is not a difficult procedure. Reducing the time of the
ginal project is the key to improved productivity. We can produce

lems as they arise, instead of waiting for the nex
other two trips to the West Coast may produce
higher quality products, and even reduce the ov
in an engineering project. Thus, a negative ca
positive when viewed from the proper perspectiv
user's point of view. Helping the user see the neg
is an important role of the system manager.

Another major point that must be addressed i
initial installations, a system administrator joi
ence to help ease the discomfort of using the syste
did not have to teach new users how to master tl
The administrator assists with suggestions on th
that best fit teleconferencing, and guides the user
sary steps. Therefore, we do not burden the user w
ity of the system in the beginning sessions. We
then, as they become more involved, and adjust
have found that we almost have to hold them back
operating it.

The system administrator and the project mana
derstand the technical aspects. This aids in the
teleconference. They know how to operate the sy
easy for the user. This is an especially importan
sional users.

After a person uses the system a few times, the un
begin to emerge. We see increased usage leading
another. One person in the department says, "(
today, guess who I talked with?" They describe
with the system, its benefits and disadvantages th
with their co-workers. The pressure of the "I did it
done it yet" attitude has helped foster increased us
This is one of the hidden benefits that we did no
beginning, or, if we did recognize it, we did not kno
deal with it. We now encourage the users to g
departments, or into other departments, and disc
ing, both audio and video. They are encouraged
wrong with the system, what improvements are r
we can do to make their communications easier. T
assist us in helping complete their work in a mor
Once again, productivity improves.

As the unexpected benefits emerged, managemen

Estimated Productivity Improvement Scale

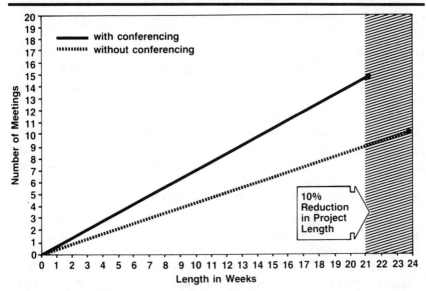

Fig. 4-7 Video teleconferencing fosters more frequent interaction and, thus, shorter decision cycles.

better products in a shorter period of time, all through increased information flow. The users again are asked to pay for the use of the system. Thus, if they are willing to bear the expenses for teleconferencing, then it must be worth it.*

The difficult measure is putting a definable dollar value on each of the engineers who attend a teleconference. Another difficult point to evaluate is whether the engineer made a better decision, or a more timely decision, based on the use of the equipment. These questions must be reversed. The engineer must explain if he made a better decision, or if the information provided was on a more timely basis and was available to him as a result of the teleconference. This kind of information can be gathered through surveys and personal interviews and measured by the increased usage of the system.

The system, however, must be billed to the users. If the cost of using the

---

* There are many variables associated with calculating the effect of teleconferencing. For the purpose of this chapter, we are only addressing the reduction of project length. This time reduction can be related to problem solving. The question still to be answered is "Does this reduction in time relate to productivity?"

system is reasonable and the equipment costs are amortized over five years, then the decision to use the system could come down to a financial one — do I travel, or do I teleconference? A review of the expenses for both meeting methods will help justify the best method (See Figure 4-8).

It is like owning a car. If we all had to sit down and cost-justify our cars based on green dollars only, we probably would not own one. However, the uses and cost justification come from finding out what you can do with a car, where you can go and what you can see. You find your own cost justification for use of the car more quickly through its use, not its cost. The same principle applies to teleconferencing equipment. You must be able to look beyond the question of how to pay for $20,000 worth of equipment. You must look at the uses and better information flow. Once you get past the hard dollars and into the soft dollars, the major cost justifications are apparent.

One of the simplest ways to measure this productivity improvement is through travel and meeting logs — watching the volume of both travel and meetings. The travel may not go down but the number of participants in a meeting may increase, as may the number of meetings. So keep a meeting log, not just a travel log, and compare how many meetings were necessary to accomplish the same task before teleconferencing was used and see what the results were. If, in the past, five face-to-face meetings were needed and now only three face-to-face meetings and two teleconferences required, we have a measure of productivity improvement. The overall budget will have decreased (if measured on an attendance basis), and more persons will have been involved. We also find that the average length of the teleconferences is shorter than the face-to-face meetings requiring travel.

Another decision that must be made in the cost-justification and measurement is whether to use teleconferencing or traveling for a face-to-face meeting. Many articles have been written on this subject. I concur with most of them. Most first meetings — first introduction meetings and sales calls meetings — are not the kind of meetings that you want to conduct with slow-scan video teleconferences. Those types of meetings need to be face-to-face, as do labor negotiations and purchasing. However, there are certain types of meetings that lend themselves well to the graphic and teleconferencing environment:

• planning,

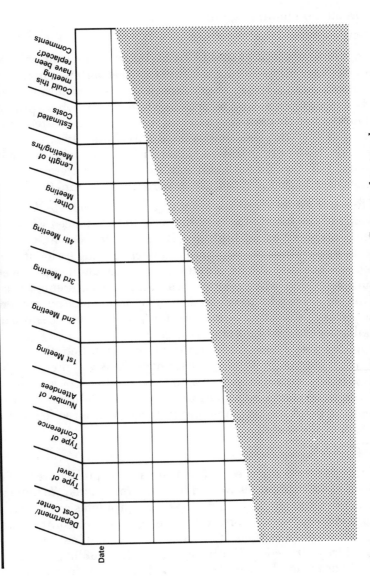

Fig. 4-8 A page from Gould's Travel and Meeting Log used to track

- implementation,
- scheduling,
- production planning, and
- engineering detail meetings.

Any routine meetings that transmit information from one person to the next are prime candidates for video teleconferencing. Instead of time consuming travel, the user projects his information, concludes his teleconference, and returns to work. This is where productivity improvement is gained — more information transmitted, more decisions made, and less time wasted traveling. Thus, as stated previously, better organization of material results in increased productivity. What we do with slow-scan video teleconferencing is make that information available in a more timely manner for the user.

The same kinds of criteria should be used for audio teleconferences. Many of the face-to-face meetings could be replaced with an audio teleconference using high quality audio equipment. An internal meeting administrator/planner can help managers identify when a face-to-face meeting is required, when an audio-only meeting is sufficient, and when a slow-scan video teleconference is required. This person can help even when a full motion video teleconference is necessary. A meeting administrator/planner, can be trained in the skills necessary to match the type of meeting to be held with the applications. The administrator/planner can help the user decide the best means for holding the meeting. This will increase the overall efficiency of all meetings with the company. The systems coordinator, or systems administrator, may also function as a central clearing point for keeping detailed records required for cost justification of the systems.

SUMMARY

This chapter is directed at the basic areas of teleconferencing. We pointed out difficulties we had in communications. We have walked through what Gould is doing to resolve problems and increase productivity by exploiting the technologies of teleconferencing. We enhanced our channels of communications and installed a network to address the cost-effectiveness and the mobility of our people. Gould searched for quality ways to transmit information to more people on a more timely basis.

We also looked into how the system was integrated, and the need for compatibility and standardization. We addressed the needs of high quality audio and why it is important for the user to have quality equipment to properly do his job.

We looked at the in-house selling process — how to get the user involved in the decision making process, all the way from the beginning, when a problem was first identified by him. Users resolve their problems, help install the solution and use the system to resolve the problem. Therefore, the users are part of the problem/solution cycle.

We talked about the need to measure productivity, both in terms of real dollars and non-real dollars, or soft dollars. We talked about the development of telecommunications and video teleconferencing throughout Gould, and how our internal information age has dictated our need and acceptance of slow-scan video teleconferencing. The success and benefits gained have led to a decision to review the entire network for expansion to 12-18 units by the end of 1984. These would be placed strategically throughout the United States to match the existing communications channels that have been identified. The development of slow-scan video teleconferencing does not preclude the development of complementary projects:

- expansion of electronic mail;
- expansion of audio teleconferencing; and
- introduction of computer conferencing.

Gould is also exploring the interactive graphics of computer conferencing, where two or more users can access the same data base and simultaneously work and communicate on projects. This new form of teleconferencing will assist the geographically dispersed engineers working on the same computer-aided design (CAD) system to solve a mutual problem. They may even document their conclusions through an interactive electronic mail system associated with the same computer conference. Future developments for video teleconferencing are in the area of compressed video, within the 1.544 Mbps and the 0.75 Mbps range. While these areas are not currently cost-justified within Gould, they may fit into our environment in the next 3-5 years.

Gould's direction has been somewhat conservative. Its needs have been identified, and equipment has been found to fit the immediate requirements. Now there is in place an "upward migration" strategy for the systems which will assist the company in reaching the stated business goals. The long-range teleconferencing strategy will involve the user as part of the plan. By retaining this important element, the strategy will continue to be successful.

THE AUTHOR

John R. Hart is Director, Corporate Telecommunications, for Gould, Inc. He is responsible for strategic planning for voice and data telecommunications, network design and equipment evaluation, electronic mail system networks, and teleconferencing networks.

Mr. Hart joined Gould in 1979 as the Manager, Corporate Telecommunications, where he became involved with all facets of corporate-wide planning for telecommunications products and services.

Mr. Hart has a B.A. from William Jewel College. He is Vice President (and President-Elect) of the Chicago Industrial Communications Association, Inc. (CICA), and is a recognized leader in the telecommunications industry, serving as both a seminar leader and guest speaker for many organizations.

Greater Southeast Community Hospital
1310 Southern Avenue, S.E.
Washington, D.C. 20032

Messrs. Brown and Levy have implemented a slow-scan video teleconferencing system at Greater Southeast Community Hospital which transmits radiology images over dial-up telephone lines to on-call radiologiest in the Washington, D.C. area. They explain the methodology and its advantages for the patient and the physician. This case is quite different from those already discussed because it is much more time sensitive.

Chapter 5

Utilizing Teleradiology to Increase the Efficiency of the Care Delivery Process

David Brown, MBA and James D. Levy, M.D., MBA

INTRODUCTION AND BACKGROUND

Greater Southeast Community Hospital is a 450-bed community hospital with an affiliated teaching program located in Washington, D.C. The hospital serves the southeast Washington area and the southern portion of Prince Georges County, Maryland. Approximately 16,000 patients per year are hospitalized at Greater Southeast Community Hospital and more than 55,000 people are treated in the facility's emergency room. The hospital provides a full range of clinical services and all medical specialties are represented on the medical staff.

Greater Southeast Community Hospital is considered to be an innovator in the use of new information technology in the hospital setting. Various computer applications have been operational since the hospital opened seventeen years ago and a continuous process of system modernization has maintained the hospital's "state-of-the-art" capability. The hospital is in the final stage of implementing the IBM Patient Care System which completely automates the institution's clinical order and report generation process. By linking all the hospital's nursing units with the ancillary services departments, this system has completely revolutionized the manner in which information is communicated throughout the hospital. A program to coordinate this system with community-based physicians' offices is being completed in another attempt to improve the efficiency of the health care delivery process. Given these undertakings, the implementation of a teleradiology system was a natural development for Greater Southeast Community Hospital.

Greater Southeast Community Hospital's Department of Radiology has been continually upgraded over the years to ensure that the department's physical plant is technologically modern. Eleven radiological suites, a nuclear medicine laboratory, a computerized tomography suite, and a recently renovated ultrasound complex are available 24 hours a day, 7 days a week. A digital angiography suite complements the department's diagnostic capabilities. The volume of testing performed by the department is approximately 100,000 studies per year with a recent trend away from standard radiographic and fluoroscopic work and an increase in special procedures.

The interests of the radiologists stimulate the hospital's Department of Radiology to adopt new technology as a means of improving the efficiency of its operations. As noted, a digital angiography system was installed recently. A dedicated department telephone system obtained more than 10 years ago improved the community's access to the department. When the hospital installed the IBM clinical management information system, the Department of Radiology was the first ancillary department to be linked with the nursing units. It was not surprising that the radiologists unanimously agreed to experiment with video teleconferencing.

TELERADIOLOGY

Teleradiology is the transmission of X-ray images from one geographic area, where a radiologist is not available, to a receiving site in another location where a radiologist is present by using telephone lines or another form of electronic transmission. The purpose of teleradiology is to use most effectively the services of radiologists.

The teleradiology application described in this chapter makes use of conventional X-ray film, a slow-scan television system, and telephone lines. Looking to the future, one can see that teleradiology will be clearly compatible with the movement toward using digital representation of a medical image. The literature suggests that digital radiographic imaging will become increasingly widespread because this technique has significant advantages over traditional film use. These advantages include reduced storage needs and reduced costs.

It is generally perceived that teleradiology will have its greatest application in linking rural areas with locations where radiologists are readily available. The recent MITRE Corporation Teleradiology Field Trial of 1982 studied this type of application and reported positively on the utility of an on-line system. The experience related in this chapter supports the MITRE findings and offers an alternative methodology, slow-scan, which deserves further evaluation and application.

THE GREATER SOUTHEAST COMMUNITY HOSPITAL TELERADIOLOGY SYSTEM

Rationale to Develop System

Greater Southeast Community Hospital radiologists are present in the department from 8:00 a.m. to 11:00 p.m., 7 days a week. On a weekly rotation, a radiologist is on-call between 11:00 p.m. and 8:00 a.m. The radiologist responds to all requests to read and interpret an emergency radiology procedure, which is usually required as the result of a trauma patient's arrival in the facility's busy emergency department. Given the high volume of motor vehicle accidents and violence-related trauma in the hospital's immediate area, there is a demand for approximately 7 nuclear medicine procedures or CT scans between 11:00 p.m. and 8:00 a.m. each week. As a result, the services of the on-call radiologist, including travel time, are required, on the average, for two hours each night.

In evaluating the types of services provided by the on-call radiologists, it became clear that invasive radiological special procedures are rarely required during the night. In effect, the only service provided by the radiologists, at this time of day, was reading a film of a study performed by a radiology technologist. As a result, when Greater Southeast Community Hospital administration and radiologists became aware of the availability and the capabilities of a teleradiology system, they made a decision to install a system which would obviate the need for a radiologist to drive to the hospital after 11:00 p.m. solely to read a film of a patient who had received a CT or a nuclear medicine scan.

System Design

The technology that makes possible the telemedicine system is an electronic concept known as the *scan conversion process*. The Robot Research scan converter equipment used by Greater Southeast Community Hospital converts to audio frequency tones — either video signals from a CT scan computer output, or TV signals from a standard closed-circuit television camera viewing an X-ray on a lightbox. The audio tones — each tone representing the brightness of a single picture dot or picture sample — are transmitted over voice-grade telephone circuits to the receiving location.* The receiving scan converter reverses the process of encoding the TV picture signals by decoding each audio frequency tone into its related electrical voltage representing the original brightness level of the transmitted video picture. Each voltage value is then translated into its equivalent binary word and stored in the scan converter's digital memory. The standard closed-circuit TV monitor at the receive location displays the received and reconstructed video image by responding to a high-speed readout of the scan converter's memory.

The main advantage of converting video signals to audio tones and *vice versa* is to make it possible to transmit and receive pictures over voice-grade communication links, such as the telephone line. Because of their narrow bandwidth, voice-grade channels can carry signals all over the world at low cost. Conventional TV, requiring a much wider video bandwidth, is restricted primarily to private network communication paths. The main limitation in sending video pictures over voice-grade channels is the increased time required to transmit each picture. Conventional TV sends many frames per second, making it possible to create the illusion of motion. Phone line television requires several seconds to convey each picture, depending on the resolution desired. The result is a sequence of "stills" or frozen pictures.

System Use

Prior to using the system, the representative from the company which installed the teleradiology equipment met individually with each of the radiologists who would be "taking call." Each radiologist was trained extensively to use the system, and learned what to do in the event of a system failure. In addition, a detailed instruction manual was prepared for the radiologists' reference. This guide was thought to be especially important given that a radiologist is only on-call once every 11 weeks.

On Monday of each week, the teleradiology receiving instrument is turned over to the radiologist who is taking call for the week. The on-call radiologist is responsible for transporting the unit, packaged in two suitcase-like containers, to his home. The system takes approximately 10 minutes to set-up and test — normally the extent

---

*For a more detailed discussion, see the following chapter entitles "Utilizing Freeze-Frame Video Technology in Telemedicine Over Voice Grade Line."

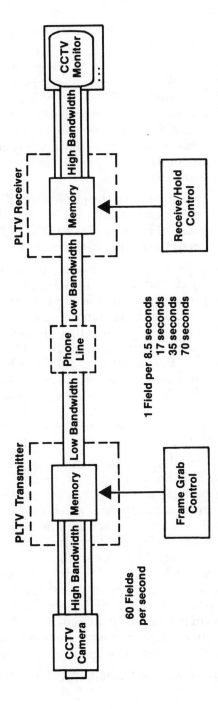

Fig. 5-1 Block diagram of scan conversion process. Video signals from a computer output or TV signal from a camera viewing an x-ray are converted to audio tones, which are transmitting over voice-grade phone lines to the receiving location, where the process of coding is reversed.

of the technical maintenance for the week, barring any unforeseen equipment malfunctions.

On the average, the teleradiology system is employed once per evening, 7 nights per week. When the emergency room physicians decide a patient needs a sophisticated radiographic procedure, they phone the on-call radiologist and also the patient's attending physician to discuss the case and determine the most appropriate radiographic test. If the physicians decide to perform a special procedure (e.g., digital angiography or an arteriogram), the radiologist must go to the hospital to perform the study.

After the technologist has positioned the patient for the procedure, he will telephone the radiologist to inform him that the study is about to begin. At this point, the radiologist and the technician will coordinate the activation of the teleradiology system.

Once an image has been obtained, it will be transmitted from Greater Southeast Community Hospital to the radiologist's home for his examination and interpretation. From this point on, the radiologist and the technician are in continuous communication until the radiologist is satisfied that the procedure has produced all of the information needed to assist in treating the patient. Once the procedure has been completed, the radiologist calls the hospital and reports his findings to the attending physician and to the emergency room. The radiologist will re-read the films in person on the following day.

System Performance

Our evaluation of the teleradiology system currently used at Greater Southeast Community Hospital is completely positive. The radiologists unanimously agree the teleradiology system is one of the most useful technological innovations to be applied to the practice of radiology in the past five years. The system has been in place at Greater Southeast Community Hospital for almost three years and has resulted in approximately 1,000 fewer nighttime visits to the department by the on-call radiologists. Theoretically, assuming an average round trip travel time of one hour, almost 1,000 travel hours have been avoided. The benefit to the radiologists plainly is evident. The teleradiology system is of significant benefit to the patient as well. The patient benefits when the radiologist can review the scans at home because the half-hour one-way travel delay is eliminated.

As indicated, the Greater Southeast Community Hospital system is used only to transmit CT and nuclear medicine scan images. Standard X-ray films are read by the emergency room physicians and re-read the following day by the radiologists. The radiologists have not been satisfied with the quality of the transmitted image of a standard X-ray, nor do they feel the need to read them because of the extensive qualifications of the emergency room physicians.

Over the past three years, approximately 1,000 patients have been evaluated using the hospital's teleradiology system and there has not yet been a single case where a diagnosis was made mistakenly from a transmitted medical image. While the radiologists feel the resolution of the transmitted image is not ideal using the slow-scan approach, only infrequently have they identified subtle findings when they re-read the original films. Almost all of the technical problems experienced with the system have been attributed to operator error and all of the radiologists agree the system performance has been exceptional. The Greater Southeast Community Hospital project has no negative experiences to report.

THE FUTURE OF THE SYSTEM

Teleradiology is a technology which has unlimited potential for the future. However, before new applications are implemented, additional developmental work needs to be completed.

As far as Greater Southeast Community Hospital is concerned, the first subject to be addressed in the future is whether the current use of a slow-scan television monitor should be replaced by a digital image transmission system. The hospital's radiologists agree with the findings of the MITRE Corporation that images transmitted by slow-scan television lack a certain degree of detail and resolution and that the system is somewhat cumbersome and slow. However, given that a higher resolution system could cost more than three times the $14,000 invested in the Greater Southeast Community Hospital system, we have concluded that a higher resolution cannot be justified at this time.* As such, hospitals and other users of slow-scan television technology should assess whether or not this medium provides all of the capabilities they require.

Regardless of which system transmits radiographs, future applications will require improved image resolution. With image resolution enhancement comes the capability to expand the types of images

---

*For a complete cost breakdown, see Chapter 5.

which can be transmitted — for example, ultrasound and other radiology specialties. Naturally, a thorough cost/benefit analysis should be conducted before more sophisticated systems are adopted. Clearly, the most obvious future use of teleradiology will be to link communities without a sufficient base of radiologists to more adequately staffed medical centers. Greater Southeast Community Hospital is completing arrangements to add a mobile radiology service to its telemedicine program. A vehicle the size of a moving van will be converted into a radiology suite equipped with a CT scanner, nuclear medicine equipment, and other radiology devices. The mobile radiology suite will be driven by a radiology technician to towns in rural southern Maryland. The radiology images taken during a procedure will be transmitted back to Greater Southeast Community Hospital to be interpreted by a hospital radiologist.

Radiologist-to-radiologist communication will also become more common in the future as radiologists become even more subspecialized. In addition, cardiac and other types of scanning techniques may become appropriate image transmission vehicles. As the practice of medicine becomes more and more complex, the cost-effectiveness of transmitting information between different areas will increase.

The Greater Southeast Community Hospital's experience with teleradiology has been extremely successful. With little capital expenditure, they have achieved a very significant, time-saving impact. We are confident that this technology will become increasingly useful as the health care industry moves into the deregulated "competitive" era that the next few years will bring.

THE AUTHORS

David Brown has served as Vice-President, Professional Services at Greater Southeast Community Hospital since 1982. In that capacity, he has made numerous contributions in corporate administration, strategic planning, and financial management. In previous work engagements, Mr. Brown served as Executive Director of Prince George's Foundation for Medical Care in Landover, Maryland, as Management Consultant to Professional Health Services in Washington, D.C., and as Hospital Management Resident for the Massachusetts Hospital School in Canton, Massachusetts.

Mr. Brown has contributed numerous articles in the health care administration field to *Quality Review Bulletin, Hospitals*, and *Hospital Peer Review*. He received his MBA in 1976 from Boston

University for Health Care Management Specialization, and earned a B.A. in 1974 from Boston University.

Dr. James D. Levy is Acting Medical Director at D.C. Village, a 530-bed long term care facility, where he has served since March 1982. Previously, Dr. Levy was Vice President for Professional Affairs at Greater Southeast Community Hospital. Before joining Greater Southeast Community Hospital, he was in private practice in internal medicine and clinical immunology in Clinton, Maryland. His earlier experience was at Prince George's General Hospital and at Walter Reed Army Medical Center.

Dr. Levy is a member of the Medical Advisory Committee for Dyatron Corporation and has served as a member of the Board of Directors of numerous health care related organizations. He has been awarded numerous fellowships and honors.

Dr. Levy earned his MBA from Loyola College in Columbia, Maryland in 1982. He completed his medical education at the University of Oregon School of Medicine in Portland, Oregon in 1969, earning an M.D. degree. His undergraduate work at the University of Oregon in Eugene, Oregon led to a B.S. degree in 1968. He has published frequently in a wide variety of medical journals and health care administration periodicals.

Building on the previous chapter, Mr. Munsey provides a conceptual explanation of the technology underlying slow-scan video teleconferencing, and in particular, teleradiology. He carefully explains the tradeoffs between speed and picture resolution, provides a clear understanding of slow-scan conversion processes, and then shows how these concepts can be practically applied to radiology problems. He completes his essay with a discussion of the training, management, and economics of slow-scan teleradiology.

Chapter 6
Utilizing Freeze-Frame Video Technology
in Telemedicine Over Voice Grade Lines
Wallace Munsey

In the last chapter, we learned how Greater Southeast Community Hospital is benefitting from the use of freeze-frame video technology applied to teleradiology. Now we will examine the techniques of using freeze-frame video over voice-grade lines from a more global and technical viewpoint. This chapter will explain how the image is scanned and converted to audio tones for transmission over voice-grade telephone lines. The lessons provided here go beyond teleradiology and telemedicine. The technological discussion and economics of freeze-frame video are applicable to any freeze-frame video teleconferencing application.

RESOLUTION VS. SPEED TRADEOFFS

Ordinary telephone lines are designed to transmit data at a rate sufficient to support voice communications. Full-motion television transmission requires several hundred ordinary voice-grade circuits. However, it is possible to transmit video images over one voice-grade telephone line by viewing one still video image at a time. Each video image requires a number of seconds (up to a minute, or longer) of transmission time. (Full-motion television is achieved by viewing 30 discrete video images per second.)

The user of video images transmitted over voice-grade phone lines would like to receive high resolution images in the shortest possible time. Unfortunately, these two aspects of phone line video images are inversely related. A high resolution video image is achieved by resolving the image to be transmitted into a large number of samples (picture elements or pixels) and transmitting the resulting data stream of pixels at a reasonably slow rate. If the number of pixels per image is reduced and/or the speed of transmitting the pixel stream is increased, the received image will be obtained in a shorter time, but the resolution of the image will be degraded. A third factor in video image resolution is the number of shades of gray (for a black-and-white image) each pixel can be assigned. An image made of pixels that vary over 64 possible shades of gray will have much better resolution than the same image transmitted using only 16 shades of gray.

The *de facto* standard for phone line video transmission is an image composed of 65,536 pixels, 64 shades of gray, and a transmission time of 35 seconds. The so-called 35-second picture has a resolution approximating that of closed-circuit television. A higher resolution image could be obtained by transmitting more pixels at the same rate or by transmitting the same number of pixels at a slower rate. For example, doubling the number of pixels (from 65,536 to 130,672) would yield a slightly higher resolution picture, but at the expense of doubling the transmission time to 70 seconds. A picture of nearly the same improved resolution could also be obtained by keeping the same number of pixels (65,536), but by halving the pixel transmission rate (from 1969 pixels per second down to 984 pixels per second). The picture transmission time again would be doubled to 70 seconds.

The utility of the 70-second phone line video image is limited. For viewing "normal scenery," the improved resolution over the 35-second frame would not be noticeable. However, character legibility of graphics is significantly enhanced by the 70-second picture.

Phone line video images can also be transmitted every 17 seconds or every 8½-seconds. The 17-second picture is slightly degraded in resolution from the 35-second picture, but it has a wide variety of application in video teleconferencing ("people" pictures) and remote surveillance. The 8½ second picture, with still further degradation in resolution, is widely used in security monitoring and telemetry. The 17-second resolution picture has one-half the number of pixels as the 35-second picture. The 8½-second picture has the same number of pixels as the 17-second picture, but the pixel transmission rate is doubled to 3,937 pixels per second.

The transmission of radiographic images over voice-grade telephone circuits is usually done at the 35-second speed. Greater detail in a small area of interest can be achieved by "zooming-in" the TV camera lens on the portion of the scan or film to be examined. As a rule, radiologists do not find the minor improvement in resolution obtained from a 70-second transmission sufficient to justify the additional time. The 17-second transmission speed is useful for screening nuclear medicine and ultrasound images. If a closer look at a scan or image is necessary, it can be retransmitted at the 35-second speed.

VIDEO SCAN CONVERSION PROCESS

During the 1970s, development in solid state electronics technology — principally digital integrated circuits — and changes in government regulation of the use of telephone lines made it possible to transmit video images on voice-grade telephone lines. The process of taking one image from a conventional TV camera, transmitting it over the telephone line, and displaying it on a conventional TV monitor is known as the *scan conversion* process. Full-motion TV is *fast scan TV* since 30 images per second are scanned onto the viewing monitor. Video transmitted over one voice-grade telephone circuit can be considered freeze-frame video since only one image is scanned onto the viewing monitor over a period of several seconds to a minute, or longer. The equipment that accomplishes the scan conversion process is appropriately termed a scan converter — more commonly known as a freeze-frame TV unit.

The scan converter at the transmit site "frame grabs" one image from the video source, converts it to a digital format, and stores it in a digital memory. The number of digital samples of the analog video image will determine the size of digital memory required and the resolution of the reconstructed image. Each digital sample of the analog signal from the video source is a picture element, or a pixel. The number of binary bits making up each digital sample (or pixel) will determine the number of possible shades of gray that can be encoded. If the digital sample contains 6 binary bits, the pixel can assume one of 64 shades of gray since 2 raised to the sixth power is 64. The so-called 35-second picture referred to in the previous section contains 256 scan lines and 256 pixels per scan line, and each pixel is a 6-bit binary word. Thus, the 35-second picture contains 256 x 256 pixels (65,536) times 6 bits per pixel for a memory requirement of 393,216 bits. Frame-grabbing one field of a video image into a digital memory requires one sixtieth of a second.

Each pixel of the stored video image is sequentially read from the scan converter memory and converted into an audio tone that is proportional to the shade of gray of that pixel. A white pixel would be represented by a 2300 hertz (Hz) tone, a black pixel by a 1500 Hz tone. The other 62 intervening shades of gray would be assigned audio tones between these two values.

The single video image is now a stream of audio tones. These tones are transmitted over the phone line and received by a scan converter unit. The receiving scan converter "reconverts" the stream of binary words (pixels) and stores them in the digital memory. The digital memory is "read out" at a high speed. The digital stream of pixels is converted back to video analog signals and fed to the conventional TV monitor for display.

The scan conversion process and scan converter performance discussed above are representative of scan conversion equipment presently on the market. It is reasonable to expect improvements in both image resolution and in image transmit time for units that will be available as narrowband video technology matures. However, as long as the voice-grade telephone circuit serves as the communications link, there are some fundamental limitations to contend with that will limit further scan conversion performance improvements where the complete image must be transmitted (as is the case with teleradiology).

TELERADIOLOGY SYSTEM CONFIGURATION CONSIDERATIONS

Each teleradiology system can be thought of as having two categories of components: system core components and system specific components. System core components are the teleradiology scan converter (TSC), the teleradiology control panel (TCP), a teleradiology telephone set (normal telephone), and a video viewing monitor. System specific components refer to those components required to provide a source of video input to the teleradiology system as well as optional video and audio recorders.

Five typical teleradiology system configurations are:

- Receive only — The teleradiology system may be used for receiving purposes only (e.g., a radiologist at home on night call). The receive-only teleradiology system configuration would require only the system core components (TSC, TCP, telephone, and monitor).

- Computer video image output — In some teleradiology system applications, the video input is from a medical diagnostic imaging system with computer-generated video images. The system configuration would be the same as a receive-only type with the addition of a coaxial cable connection from the imaging system video output.

- TV camera generated image — Teleradiology systems that involve transmission from a film lightbox set-up will require a standard TV camera (either wall or tripod mounted) to be connected to the teleradiology scan converter (TSC). Other components would be the same as the receive-only teleradiology system configuration.

- Multiple video sources — A teleradiology system can be configured to accept radiographic outputs from several sources (e.g., outputs from CT scanner and ultrasound as well as from TV camera for lightbox viewing). The several video sources are routed to a video switcher, that connects with the TSC. The controls of the switcher are added to the TCP.

- Multipurpose system — A teleradiology system can be used in general telemedicine applications such as continuing medical education (CME), consultation, transmission of instrumentation readouts (EKG and other waveform readings), and administrative and technical teleconferencing meetings. System specific components required for multipurpose applications would be determined from detailed requirements of the intended use. The teleradiology scan converter is fully capable of supporting all of the above applications. However, additional controls may have to be provided for a separate, all purpose, remote control unit that would be exchanged with the TCP for non-teleradiology system uses.

TV Camera Generated Image

Some planning is required to obtain the configuration of the TV camera lightbox arrangement. The first thought is usually to use wall-mounted lightboxes common to radiology reading rooms. However, this arrangement requires a stationary source film and a moving camera. When the camera is moved from an over-view of the entire film are, to a smaller portion for a close-up, additional refocusing and zooming time are required, and operator frustration can be quite high. With a horizontal lightbox and a stationary, vertically-mounted TV camera, the source film can be easily and quickly moved to the desired position while the camera lenses are being adjusted.

The TV camera should be a good quality (600 lines or greater resolution), two-thirds inch separate mesh vidicon tube. The higher cost, low light level cameras require higher cost lenses to accommodate the bright light source of the lightbox. The higher cost, one-inch separate mesh vidicon camera gives more performance than is needed by the scan converter video processing circuits. (Cameras with vidicon tubes do require special operating precautions in order to avoid the "burn-in problem.")

The use of fixed focal length lenses is not recommended since the camera will have to be moved when the area of the film to be transmitted is made smaller or larger. The 18-108 mm, one inch, medium speed, manual zoom lens seems to be a well-balanced choice in cost, resolution, performance, flexibility, and ease of use considerations.

The TV monitor should be a 9-or-12 inch size cathode ray tube (CRT) with a minimum resolution of 750 lines in the center. Monitor size is primarily determined by average viewing distance. If the operator preview monitor is close to the camera lightbox set-up, a 5-inch monitor could be used. For "across the room" viewing, a 17- or 19-inch monitor would be suitable.

Computer Video Image Output

It will not be possible in all cases to connect the video output of medical diagnostic imaging equipment with the scan converters used in teleradiology systems. The video format of the medical video output must be the same format as that used in the scan converter. The conventional 525-line composite video is used by nearly all ultrasound and nuclear medicine equipment and in early generation CT scanners. Late model CT scanners use a higher resolution video format that is not compatible with the scan converters currently on the market.

GREATER SOUTHEAST COMMUNITY HOSPITAL TELERADIOLOGY SYSTEM

The teleradiology system now operating at Greater Southeast Community Hospital is configured along the lines of the TV camera generated image described above. The lightbox is horizontal and the camera is placed on a vertical wall mount. A close-up lens is attached to the front of the manual zoom lens, and the lightbox to camera distance is approximately 27 inches. This arrangement and equipment permits the operator to frame and transmit a 14-inch by 17-inch chest X-ray or a detail of a CT scan as small as 2 inches wide.

The 9-inch operator preview monitor is placed in a position that permits the operator to compare readily the image in the TV monitor with the lightbox image to insure that the proper video adjustments are made before the picture is transmitted. The scan converter is directly below the lightbox. While the contrast and brightness controls on the scan converter should rarely be adjusted, they should be readily available for unusually bright or dark films.

The telephone set used to connect the scan converter to the telephone line should be close to the scan converter and to the other elements of the system. Most teleradiology transmissions can be conducted with only one phone line. The phone line can be used alternately for the video transmission with no voice possible, and for voice transmission with no video possible. An automatic switching between video and voice (such as is available on the Greater Southeast Community Hospital scan converter) is highly recommended. A second telephone line is also required to facilitate radiologist-to-radiologist consultations between hospitals or between office and hospital. Conversations can be continued over the voice telephone circuit while the scanned image is being transmitted on the video telephone circuit. The two telephone circuits for the teleradiology system should be unswitched, dedicated lines that are independent of the hospital communications system. This arrangement ensures a stronger and cleaner signal, facilitates rapid communications, and removes the inevitable interruptions common to large institutional telecommunications systems.

Although not installed in the Greater Southeast Community Hospital teleradiology system, a speakerphone would be useful during teleradiology transmissions. Several participants could be involved in the discussions, and the operator could be more efficient in preparing and transmitting each video image.

Teleradiology system physical security was considered during the planning phase since TV cameras, lenses, and TV monitors are attractive items and relatively easy to remove. The Greater Southeast Community Hospital system is installed in a radiology reading room that is always locked when not in use by a responsible member of the staff. For installations in non-secure areas, alarmed electrical plug-in adapters which will issue a loud noise if the units are unplugged or if the power cords are cut are available.

TRAINING, TROUBLE SHOOTING, AND SERVICE

Initial training is important for radiologists and technicians to gain confidence in the teleradiology system's capability to perform its job. Self-training could lead to improper use and ultimately to the abandonment of the system. The training session should include three main topics:

- Equipment operating procedures;

- Phone line protocol for transmitting images over one phone line shared with voice transmission; and

- Technique for adapting camera lens, viewing monitor, and scan converter controls to obtain quality images for transmission.

After-hours or weekend sessions might have to be scheduled to ensure that all system users have had an opportunity to work with the system. A simplified step-by-step procedure sheet should be the basis of training. This sheet should be posted near the system so it can be used as an operating guide.

Errors in system hookup for portable systems and operating errors will be common in the early phases of use of a teleradiology system. The impact of such errors can be greatly reduced by insisting on complete system documentation in clear, lay terms. The documentation must include complete and clearly worded trouble-shooting flow charts. The user should be able to recognize the symptom and apply the remedy by following the chart.

It is equally important that the system installer is available by telephone for system trouble-shooting support around the clock for the first few months after the system is operational. Service availability afterward can be negotiated as required.

If the hospital has a video equipment service and a repair capability, it should not be necessary to have a service contract with an outside agency. The teleradiology system is essentially a closed circuit television system with the exception of the scan converter and telephone hookup. Competent local repair and service of the scan converter should be available when support on that part of the system is required.

TELERADIOLOGY SYSTEM COST ESTIMATING

The basic cost of a hospital teleradiology system should be between $7,500 and $9,500. This would include equipment costs for the scan converter, camera and lens, preview monitor, and system control unit. Installation charges — including cable and cable routing, initial training, and on-call support — are also included in this estimate. Additional costs would be necessary for dedicated telephone lines, speakerphone, additional telephone sets, and multiple video hook-ups (CT scanner, ultrasound, or nuclear medicine video outputs, in addition to camera source for the lightbox). Conversion of a computer workstation cart to a self-contained teleradiology system cart would cost approximately $700 to $900 (including the cost of the cart, power strip, cart cables, system switch, camera stem and holder, and other such modifications for a complete set-up). Additional scan converter options (e.g., two memories) and video or audio tape recorders (freeze-frame TV can be recorded on ordinary audio tape recorders) would add still more cost and utility to the system.

A portable receive-only system for the radiologist's use at home while on-call would cost between $6,000 and $7,000. If each participating radiologist agreed to purchase a quality TV viewing monitor to keep at home (approximately $225), the portable system would be less costly (no expensive monitor carrying case) and much easier to manage and transport. Since the portable system is a receive-only system, cameras, lenses, and cabling are not required.

A receive-only teleradiology system installed in a radiologist's office should cost slightly less than a portable system. However, a dedicated telephone or a speakerphone and telephone service charges might increase the cost to about the same level as the portable unit.

Some dealers will rent the necessary components of a basic teleradiology system for a 30-, 60-, or 90-day evaluation program. Some dealers will arrange a lease-purchase plan for system purchase. In other cases, the only option might be outright purchase.

THE AUTHOR

Mr. Wallace Munsey is the founder and President of Electronic Meeting Services, an organization providing system planning and technical support to organizations preparing to acquire narrowband video systems. Formerly, he was Director of Product Development for Robot Research, Inc., the world's leading manufacturer of narrowband video transceivers — i.e., freeze-frame television. During the three years he spent with Robot Research, Mr. Munsey directed or instructed over 700 video conferences.

Prior to his work at Robot Research, Mr. Munsey was senior research analyst for System Planning Corporation in Rosslyn, Virginia. This work followed the completion of a 26-year career in the *U.S. Air Force* where he served in the rank of Colonel and was the *Deputy Director* of the B-1 Weapon Acquisition Program. He holds a B.S. *degree in Electrical* Engineering and a M.S. in Systems Management.

Although this chapter's examples bear some resemblance to the application of slow-scan video teleconferencing at Greater Southeast Community Hospital, the authors describe some unique circumstances which should not be overlooked. Unlike the teleradiology application already discussed in some detail, the Aroostook County experience is different in both application and emphasis. The authors focus on implementation issues and on some vexing problems which eventually were solved.

Chapter 7
Health Care Video Teleconferencing
in Aroostook County Maine
Judith Feinstein, Anne Niemiec, and Robert Ellis

An interesting and highly instructive use of electronic conferencing has been developing in Maine for a decade now. The experience demonstrates how relatively simple techniques can be adapted in ways which provide services of great value which would otherwise be unavailable, or available on a much more limited scale, in the remote areas being served. This chapter traces the history of the slow-scan video teleconferencing experiences of Medical Care Development, Inc. The lessons learned should be encouraging to teleconferencers in many circumstances.

Medical Care Development, Inc. (MCD), an organization devoted to the identification and resolution of problems in health care delivery in Maine, has been involved in telecommunications since the early 1970s. MCD's Blue Hill-Dear Isle Telecommunications Project connected a small hospital and a remote health care center for the purpose of facilitating ambulatory care in an area without a primary care physician. This project was in operation from 1973 to 1978 and was discontinued only after the health care center recruited a physician.

In 1976 MCD implemented a unique microwave-linked video teleconferencing and interactive telecommunications system which connected five hospitals, a family practice residency, and a University of Maine campus. The Central Maine Interactive Telecommunications System (or CMITS as it has come to be known) met a variety of needs including meetings, continuing medical education courses, nursing programs, and other educational events including programs via satellite. The system was originally funded under Exchange of Medical Information Grants from the Veterans Administration to Medical Care Development, Inc. Eventually, it became self-funded as participants were charged for services.

Because of the success of the CMITS within the central Maine area, expansion possibilities were explored for other eligible territories. It quickly became apparent that expansion of the existing broadband microwave-linked system or the construction of other such systems in other parts of Maine would be extremely expensive. It is primarily for this reason that other technologies began to be explored.

AROOSTOOK COUNTY REQUIREMENTS

Aroostook County (see Figure 7-1) was identified as an area that might benefit from a telecommunications system. This county has a population of approximately 100,000 people in an area greater than that of Connecticut and Rhode Island combined. It is isolated from the nearest urban center in the state by a 150-mile stretch of woods. Aroostook's ratio of people per square mile is about 14, which is less than one half of the 32 people per square mile for the rest of Maine.

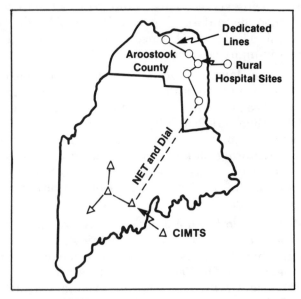

Fig. 7-1 Central Maine Interactive Telecommunications System (CMITS) is a full-motion video teleconferencing system in Southern Maine. The Aroostook County System is a slow-scan video system interconnected with the CMITS network.

Travel within Aroostook County and from Aroostook municipalities to the rest of Maine is a major undertaking. To travel from Fort Kent to Houlton requires at least two and a half hours with good weather conditions. In bad weather, the trip might not even be possible. An additional two hours must be added to a trip continuing from Houlton to the nearest urban center, Bangor. If a person were to continue to Augusta, Maine's state capital, an additional one and a half hours would be required. This means a total travel time from Fort Kent to Augusta of at least six hours and from Boulton to Augusta of at least three and a half hours.

Participation in meetings and educational activities by Aroostook health care professionals requires a substantial investment of time for travel alone. Needless to say, this places even greater stress on their understaffed health care system.

In addition to the need for education access to simply keep current with various accrediting agencies, there is a need to overcome the isolation that affects geographically separated health care professionals. A 1978 MCD survey indicated that a lack of peer contact to allay professional isolation in the rural areas was the most frequently cited problem by rural health care providers.

With all of these factors in mind, a grant was submitted to the former Department of Health, Education and Welfare (now the Department of Education) "to establish an innovative telecommunications system to serve health and educational needs of Maine's most isolated rural county."

System Design Criteria

The resulting slow-scan video teleconferencing demonstration project was to provide a telecommunications package to Aroostook County at a reasonable cost. In order to keep the cost as low as possible, three criteria were established before system design and construction were started. First, the equipment had to be "user-friendly." It became obvious when talking with the hospitals that additional personnel could not be added to run equipment at each site. Therefore, the consoles had to be designed with as few knobs and buttons as possible in order to facilitate the education of users.

Second, to reduce the cost of sophisticated bridging equipment (the equipment needed to connect 3 or more sites simultaneously on demand) that might be required, the decision was made to use a pair of dedicated, resistor-type bridges which would be housed in the

Presque Isle phone office. The connections between the hospitals and the phone company bridges were to be accomplished with a pair of dedicated phone circuits, one circuit carrying the voice audio and one circuit carrying the slow-scan audio tones.

Third, there needed to be a provision to connect the CMITS with the Aroostook County Telecommunications System using a pair of in-state WATS phone lines to allow people in central Maine to communicate with people in northern Maine. The use of dial-in ports on the bridge would allow for a much greater flexibility and would also be the least expensive option to provide an interconnect between Aroostook and central Maine.

The On-Site Equipment

As previously stated, there was a need to keep the on-site equipment as simple as possible. In addition to the personnel crunch felt by the participants, there was also a crunch on meeting room space. Therefore, whatever the package contained, it would be necessary to make it somewhat portable.

From experience gained from use of the central Maine equipment, the decision was made to place all seldomly used equipment and controls behind a panel dorr in the console. Many times there would be only a few people using the equipment. Therefore, a remote control would be needed for users to operate the camera from their seats while meeting or presenting.

Lastly, there needed to be a provision to record sessions and play back taped information.

With these areas of concern and other specifications, the bid process began. Lake Systems in Newton, Massachusetts, was the successful bidder. They chose to provide Robot freeze-frame equipment and Darome two-wire miniconveners (for the audio system). The design of the console was straightforward (see Figure 7-2). The camera was mounted on a remotely controlled pan/tilt platform. The lens had a remotely controlled iris, focus, and six-to-one zoom. The 17-inch black-and-white monitor was located in the top of the console and its controls were left exposed for easy adjustment of picture. The Darome mini-converes were adapted to a 19-inch, rack-mountable, front panel and the in-coming audio volume knob was moved from the rear to the front.

A single power switch was provided to facilitate turning the equipment on and off. The Robot slow-scan equipment and the stereo

*Fig. 7-2 The slow-scan console unit contains the camera on a re-
motely controlled pan/tilt platform, a 17-inch black-and-
white monitor, scan converter, and audio equipment.*

audio recorder were located in the bottom of the console behind a
panel door. At the bottom of the console a shallow drawer was
provided for microphone cables and other odds and ends. The four
microphones could be stored on a shelf located in the back of the
console.

The remote control box was designed to include all of the camera
functions, pan/tilt, focus, zoom, and iris, and all of the slow-scan
functions, preview, picture select, send and sending speed. The connections for the remote control box and the microphones were located on the front of the console for easy access. Generally, this arrangement has provided the system users with an easily operated,
"friendly" piece of equipment.

Troubles with the Telephone Network

All of the lines from the five sites came into the Presque Isle telephone office where they were then bridged together using two sepa-

rate passive resistor-type bridges. At first, both the audio network and the slow-scan network were identical. However, soon after getting all of the equipment on line, it became apparent that there were problems. The audio would whistle and howl and the pictures would consist of many line "drop-outs" and "echos," if they were received at all.

A major concern at this time was that the actual source of the problem was difficult to determine. The phone company was certain, at first, that the problem was in the equipment located at the sites and not in the circuits themselves. Adding to this problem was the lack of documentation which would indicate that the passive bridging arrangement would do what we expected it to do.

The MCD engineer for the project began the difficult task of getting to the root of the problem. First, he took a self-taught crash course in "telephone-ese," a special language consisting almost entirely of buzz words and code numbers. Next, he made numerous measurements throughout the system. Finally, he took these measurements to the phone company and convinced them to look again at their circuits.

The phone company people were very cooperative. They had not encountered anything similar to slow-scan before, except possibly in data circuits, and were willing to do whatever needed to be done to make the system work — within reason.

By this time, it was obvious to both the MCD engineer and the phone company people that there was a problem achieving a proper "balance" in the system when transmitting the slow-scan tones. Using the newly installed dial interface to the system, measurements were made in MCD's engineering office in Augusta, Maine, and in the telephone company's engineering office in Boston. The decision was then made to change the slow-scan network to a four-wire configuration and to use "precision termination sets" at all sites for both the voice and the slow-scan networks. This is the configuration that continues to work for us today. The major problems in the operation of the system today are either human in nature or an occasional broken microphone cable.

The difficulties explained above took about fourteen months to iron out. If the problems had continued for much longer, the project would not have survived. Luckily, the Aroostook County telecommunications System has survived technically and continues to grow in utilization.

PROCESS AND PROTOCOLS

Slow-scan teleconferencing creates a unique relationship between voice and image. They are not as tightly bound as they are over a full video communications link or a face-to-face meeting; but they can be used to supplement or counterpoint one another in novel ways. Because one does not have the continuous nonverbal feedback that is at a face-to-face meeting, one needs to do certain things differently. One's skills (or lack thereof) at conducting meetings become more obvious.

More structure is needed in running meetings on a slow-scan system. As a result, meetings tend to be shorter with more accomplished in less time. There is still some social chit-chat but less than at a face-to-face meeting. To take advantage of the psychological "presence" factors made possible by the technology, people are encouraged to send a picture when they speak.

As with a video link of any type, care must be taken to keep graphics readable. Such care usually results in more impact. While written guidelines about visuals are available, people often need to experience their importance firsthand. Examples of good visuals are an integral part of our demonstrations, so that initial planning with first-time users includes discussion of appropriate visuals which can enhance their meeting or presentation.

Disadvantages may include unseen interruptions and side conversations at sites not being heard or seen on the monitor. Careful planning and some basic protocols can help to mitigate against these sorts of disruptions. For example, the presenting speaker or meeting chairperson can "check in" with participants at regular intervals to keep them involved in the meeting. When there are several people at one site who begin discussing the business of the meeting among themselves, it is helpful if someone lets the entire group know what is going on.

IMPLEMENTATION ISSUES

The support and interest of the chief executive officers of the hospitals have been crucial to the success of this system, corroborating research in business which has demonstrated the importance of the visible involvement of top-level management in the introduction of teleconferencing. They use the system for regional administrative meetings, particularly in the winter, or for ongoing discussions of specific issues. Their support and interest demonstrates a visible commitment to employees of the hospitals.

One strategy for implementation has been to introduce new employees to the system and ask them to make short presentations, both as a way of meeting people and of introducing to others the resources they bring to the hospital. One reason for paying particular attention to new people is that there is no preconceived attitude against the system which needs to be overcome. Because of the problems and time involved with implementation, an attitude of resistance is not uncommon among some long-time employees.

As with many other new technologies, peer influence and involvement have proven to be a factor. Positive experiences help create and maintain an open attitude and enthusiasm about using the system, and encourage further exploration of its potential capabilities. Seeing peers achieve a level of comfort and competence also helps the new user gain a sense of his or her own ability to use the system.

It is clear that the first uses are also critical, as another example from the hospitals can illustrate. In the fall of 1980, a group of operating room and recovery room nurses were brought together on the system to plan a training workshop. This happened during the time before the system became fully operational. The system performed unevenly through several meetings and a majority of participants were dissatisfied. Although they did not continue to meet for some time, the planning for the workshop was accomplished through a number of small, in-person on-site meetings, involving considerably more time and travel for the workshop coordinator.

On the other side, we have the experience of the demonstration arranged for Cooperative Extension Service Staff of the University of Maine. It was a particularly interactive session in which there was no awkwardness or perception of the technology as a barrier. Verbal and visual 'exchanges were constant and there was almost the same feeling as sitting around a table.

It does take time for people to get used to the equipment. If anything goes wrong, especially the first time people use the system, then acceptance takes longer. As with many other things, where the need is greater, the resistance is less. There is a range of responses to technological difficulties. Some will react immediately, with no thought of returning, and make statements to the effect of "I knew it wouldn't work, anyway!" It may well be part of a larger attitude or fear of technology. Many times what we call a "people problem" (someone incorrectly using the equipment) is attributed to the technology. The technology gets the blame for problems, no matter what the cause, because for the casual user, it is perceived that the *system* did not work. Others, however, are able to manage the problems, and somehow accept (perhaps on faith) that the difficulties are temporary. A problem with the camera focus control during the demonstration for the Department of Education provides an example. People were obviously disappointed with the unfocused, blurry pictures, but did not dwell on the problem and went on with their business.

As part of the training process, people are encouraged to have fun with the equipment. Playing with it decreases the time it takes for people to become comfortable with the equipment and allows them to get over the initial fear of it.

ACCESS TO OTHER TELECONFERENCING RESOURCES

Most of the resources shared thus far have been local, but this slow-scan technology allows access to resources in other parts of the country using telephone lines with other locations that have robot transceivers, or to create audio-only links with any location. With this ability, we have accessed audio-only and audio-video programs from California, North Carolina, Maryland, and Illinois. Gaining access to other rural areas of the country to share problem solving methods and information is being discussed with Missouri, North Carolina, and neighboring New Brunswick.

The Aroostook County network is a member of the Association of Hospital Television Networks, a national consortium of 30 regional television networks providing educational services to staff and patients of more than 900 hospitals. Association activities include development of programming distributed nationally by satellite, developing mechanisms for sharing among member networks, and consultation with producers on educational design and network services.

Although our initial focus in northern Maine has been on slow-scan video, we are exploring a variety of technological options, realizing that different options may be more appropriate for certain needs. We are concerned with technological fit; we work with individuals and groups to choose and then effectively use the technology to meet their needs.

THE AUTHORS BIOGRAPHICAL SKETCHES

Judith A. Feinstein has been Director of Northern Maine RAISE since July of 1980. RAISE, a Regional approach to Improved Health Services through Education, is an operational program of the Main Hospital Association and is supported by the five hospitals in Aroostook County. The agency's primary mandate is to develop and coordinate continuing education opportunities for health care personnel throughout the County. Feinstein's responsibilities include overall direction for needs assessment, program implementation, and ongoing development. Prior to this position, she served as Program Manager/Critical Care with the Office of Emergency Medical Services of the Massachusetts Department of Public Health, Boston, and also worked as a program evaluator with an alcohol education program at the University of Massachusetts, Amherst. Feinstein is a graduate of Beloit College, Beloit, Wisconsin, and has a graduate degree in public health from the University of Massachusetts, Amherst.

Anne Niemiec is Director of Interactive Telecommunications Systems at Medical Care Development, Inc., a non-profit health care research and development organization based in Augusta, Maine. Her responsibilities include the management of the Central Maine Interactive Telecommunications System and the Aroostook County Telecommunications System. Previously, she was the education specialist for the Central Maine Interactive Telecommunications System. Before working at Medical Care Development, she directed a cooperative program between the City Colleges of Chicago and the Health and Hospitals Governing Commission of Cook County. Niemiec is chairman of the Board of the Association of Hospital Television Networks and is on the Board of Directors of the American Society for Healthcare Education and Training. She received her undergraduate degree in psychology from Marquette University and her master's degree in educational psychology from the University of Chicago.

Robert Ellis is Assistant Director of Telecommunications at Medical Care Development, Inc., a non-profit health care research and development organization based in Augusta, Maine. His responsibilities include managing the day to day operations of the Telecommunications System. Previously, he was in charge of Media Services at Mid-Maine Medical Center. He received his undergraduate degree from Bowdoin College and is presently enrolled in the Executive MBA program at the University of New Hampshire Whittemore School of Business.

rt The National Center of Management Studies in Human Services

Whipp and Molinaro describe their experiences in managing a one-way full-motion video teleconferencing system which they use for training throughout the USA. Some of the management issues for a one-way system are similar to bear a resemblance to the concerns already discussed. But many of the problems faced by the authors are completely unique to their technology. Arranging for satellite down-links in dozens of locations for each conference proves to be a vexing problem. Each meeting takes on the character of a new project, and project management disciplines must be applied.

Chapter 8
The Human Services Network at the West Virginia
Research and Training Center
Dave Whipp and David A. Molinaro

In 1982 the West Virginia Rehabilitation Research and Training Center aired two teleconferences via satellite for human service professionals across the country. This chapter recalls that experience and provides after-the-fact reflections.

The center, which is federally funded, is responsible for conducting research and providing training for rehabilitation professionals who work with handicapped people in all 50 states. The center has provided training via print, slides, film, video tape, audio conference, and live programs. The advent of satellite technology for training applications fell nicely within the center's interests and needs. The staff gradually dedicated more time to studying and defining this technology, which resulted in the initiation of a rehabilitation satellite network in 1982 and subsequent preparation of teleconferences for 1984. The network is called the Human Services Network (HSN). Telecast I reached 8 states, 15 sites, and 107 trainees. Telecast II reached 28 states, 35 sites, and 450 trainees. We report this experience to you in terms of human considerations, technological factors, organizational matters, a work plan, and reflections.

HUMAN FACTORS

In the relationship of people and machines, the term "human factors" often refers to the relationship's degree of comfort. This discussion will take "human factors" beyond the issue of comfort to additional motivations which prompt involvement. Understanding these motivations can help to make the experience as comfortable as possible for all persons involved.

During the course of this project we became aware that the participants had many other motivations beyond the stated purpose of providing or receiving training. We found that clarification of the goals and roles of the people involved helped us manage the project more effectively. We divide the participants into three groups: ourselves (the provider), the audience (the receiver), and the technical service providers.

The Providers

The HSN production staff members were interested, both personally and professionally, in the use of satellite technology. The staff had been involved in a number of media productions, both individually and as a group. Thus, the use of satellites was perceived as a natural outgrowth of the use of media to increase the reach of their work and to serve as a new frontier to conquer. The staff had considerable interest and expertise in education, communication, and rehabilitation. The primary reward for staff members was to be useful, professional, and first in the nation to use this technology for rehabilitation training and research.

The two program content specialists were research and training staff members. They were committed to their work, and held a strong belief in its value to the intended audience. They saw teleconferences as an opportunity to increase the reach of their work, and to impart useful skills or tools to their audience. As both specialists had feature roles in the telecasts there was even greater personal motivation to have the program be successful.

The Audience

Although the audience consisted of professionals in vocational rehabilitation, individual participants had many and varied reasons for attending. We had expected the primary goal for most of the audience would be to increase their professional status through the acquisition of new skills and knowledge. For this reason, we offered Continuing Education Units and Certified Rehabilitation Counselor Credits as official evidence of their training. Instead, as our evaluation demonstrated, the most popular reason checked for attendance was "really interested in subject." Another common reason was "encouraged by supervisor"; some people checked "required."

Beyond these reasons for attendance, trainees were also influenced by the economics (low registration fee) and the convenience (closeness to work) of the training. Having attended once, they were additionally influenced to return by the quality of the experience, the perceived value of the training, the physical comfort, the level of participation, the lack of aggravation, and the coming attractions segment of the program.

For whatever reason, they may have attended, the evaluation showed the trainees liked the experience and said they would come again. Thus, it is safe to conclude that the programs met their needs, and made them comfortable with the training medium.

The Technical Service Providers

While the satisfaction of the technical service providers may not be a primary concern in teleconferencing, we believe concern for their interests will result in a better quality production. We have found the groups and individuals from whom we purchased services are knowledgeable in their areas of expertise. We have learned that if they are given some control over the production's quality they will, in turn, respond with valuable suggestions and will put more effort into making the production "the best possible."

The three groups with whom we had the most direct experience were the crews at the Public Broadcasting Service Station where we developed the preproduced video segments, the people at the uplink studio, and those who coordinated the technology components; i.e., satellite rental, uplink, and receiving sites.

These people were professionals and contributed to the overall quality of each telecast. Experience may have taught them, however, that not everyone welcomes their suggestions because they hold back a bit until they realize that their contribution is desired. Returning as much control as possible to these technical providers enhances their sense of responsibility, and increases the quality and frequency of their contributions.

TECHNICAL FACTORS

We present technological considerations in three areas: the preproduced segments, the uplink, and the training sites.

Preproduction Site

We had two studios available to us for the development of the pretaped training segments: a small format studio which was available free of charge, and a Public Broadcasting Service (PBS) studio which was available at commercial rates (see Figure 8-1). Although material transmitted by satellite for non-broadcast purposes (such as teleconferencing) does not have to meet FCC standards, we chose to use the PBS studio for several reasons.

Fig. 8-1 A typical production set used by the Human Services Network for the preparation of preproduction training segments.

First, we believed the viewer was accustomed to a commercial television quality video, and that an inferior quality might interfere with the training. Second, through our working relationship with two PBS studios, we had learned how helpful it is to use full-time, professional camera operators, engineers, technical directors, and lighting people. They can produce superior quality material in a much shorter time than we ever could in the small format studio.

The third reason for choosing PBS, with its ability to provide broadcast quality reproduction, was our intent to market the training tapes after the broadcast. If we had produced the material on smaller format tape, edited it, and then made copies from the edited tape, there would have been a substantial decrease in quality.

The actual studio charge was about $350 per hour. We used several methods to control studio costs. We designed and constructed our own sets, we did all the scripting, and, as the script was developed in a word processor, we printed it out in the proper form for the teleprompter. We provided our own talent, director, and technical supervisor. We also had the production tapes (2-inch quadraphonic) dubbed to 3/4-inch tape and made rough edits on them, so that all time-consuming edit decisions could be made out of the studio. This edited 3/4-inch tape was then taken back to the studio where the studio staff easily assembled the final master on the larger format tape.

Origination/Uplink Site

Our choice of an uplink or broadcast facility was influenced by the following factors. We wanted an economical, full-motion video, interactive-audio, and broadcast-quality facility. The Bell & Howell studios in Washington, D.C. nicely met these needs.

Uplink facilities vary considerably in features and price. We searched for the site which could meet our needs at the lowest price. (Note that by preproducing the major training segment of the telecast, we limited the risks associated with an entirely live production.) The uplink facility that we selected provided a small studio in which the talent remained seated behind a table. Three fixed cameras pointed at the table were supplemented by one document camera, fixed lighting, and 3/4-inch video playback equipment. By planning for the constraints of the studio, we were able to make the facility serve our needs quite well.

Interactive audio allowed the trainees to interact with the content specialist during the question and answer period. A team of secretaries screened the collect calls and passed them to both the director and moderator.

The origination/uplink facility, as we learned, should also be "redundant" — that is, have the ability to reach other satellites, or use different transponders (channels) on the original satellite. The origination site that we used transported the signal to the uplink in Virginia by way of a microwave signal from D.C.

Receiving/Training Sites

Our experience led us to believe that the receiving sites were the system's "weak link" due to the time absorbed in their coordination, their high cost and, at times, their poor physical qualities. While there are many facilities available for teleconferencing, considerable work must go into locating and contracting for their services. As all negotiations take place by phone and mail, careful questioning and specification of needs are critical.

We required training sites that could receive Westar IV signals and accommodate 30 people in a comfortable environment. The sites had to be accessible for trainees using wheelchairs, and required adequate parking facilities. There needed to be enough television monitors (two) for all trainees to see properly, a telephone for the audioconference segment, and tables for small group activities and writing.

We contracted with a broker, the Public Service Satellite Consortium, to handle the majority of receiving sites; but as the network grew, we coordinated some of them ourselves for several reasons. Since much of the audience knew us, they called us instead of the broker when they wanted to join the program. Many of the sites could only accommodate a small audience which would not cover costs, and we kept their costs down by coordinating these sites ourselves.

Problems arose from the lack of consistency among the sites. There was a "mixed bag" of physical facilities. Some personnel were comfortable hosting groups; some were not. Rental rates fluctuated widely. One site was unable to aim its dish at another satellite when required and missed the entire program. Three sites could not adequately heat the training rooms, and one site (the most expensive) placed trainees in a hallway. Another used its unpainted cinderblock studio for trainees. Interestingly, the most comfortable site was the least expensive.

ORGANIZATIONAL CONSIDERATIONS

As stated earlier, the center was simply interested in adding satellite teleconferencing to its existing repertoire of diffusion techniques. To achieve this goal, a staff of four people worked more or less full-time on the network. Their respective roles were:

1. Coordinator, producer, writer.
2. Media and technology technician, carpenter.
3. Media director, set designer and artist.
4. Secretary, accountant, information coordinator.

Other staff provided consultation and support:

1. Receptionists handled calls concerning the network and programs.

2. Three secretaries assisted in bulk mailings of brochures and training materials.
3. Center administrators lent valuable support, guidance and approval to the overall plan.
4. Print staff produced promotional materials in large quantities.

Outside the center, staff were supported in each network state by local site facilitators and marketing contacts. The site facilitators, all human service professionals, handled receiving-site activities on the day of each telecast. Marketing contacts assisted the network by promoting each telecast via newsletters, professional associations, letters, phone calls, and personal contacts. In some states one person doubled as facilitator and contact.

Benefit/Cost

From the center's vantage point three clear benefits were derived from the satellite venture.

1. Information quickly reached a more varied and larger audience by satellite delivery than through other diffusion techniques.
2. The result of reaching a larger audience was a greater subsequent demand for the center's media and print products and staff consultation on the telecast subjects.
3. The network's development encouraged an educational thrust that reached funding and policy-making individuals in Washington. These significant people, now familiar with both the technology and with the Center's capacities, are more likely to support the center's efforts with funding and additional content resources.

Costs can be measured in many ways. We will take three.

Psychological Costs. The staff simply ran out of gas. There was too much to do for too few people. The newness, the thrill, the rough spots and tight scheduling all took their toll.

Opportuntiy Cost. What would the Center have lost by not doing it at all? Quite simply, we would have lost the benefits noted above.

Financial Cost. After all receipts were tabulated and bills paid, the center was "out" $7,000 dollars, a net cost to the center of $12.57 to train each of the 557 participants. As of this writing, we have not kept track of post-telecast sales of video tapes and selected printed materials which naturally lessen the out-of-pocket final costs (and eventually, will enhance the return on investment).

More On Economics

We wanted the network to either break even or, ideally, to produce surplus revenue that would finance future program production and network expansion. The tuition charge for each trainee was $45.00. Our initial effort did not leave us with any surplus.

The greatest economic burden borne by the center was the rental of receiving sites. Whether sites be Marriott Hotels, Holiday Inns, or PBS stations, their rental is very expensive — at the low end, 60% of total expenditures.

The burden may lessen, however, as receiving-only satellite dishes become more available due to their gradually decreasing price. Interested agencies and associations will be more inclined to buy their own dishes. As a result, an organization such as the center can reduce its fee for training, and concentrate primarily on identifying and producing program content for telecast to a network of dedicated rehabilitation receiving sites.

Another challenge faced by the center is to increase audience size at each receiving site. We found that we had two major items to market. Obviously, as in any training program, we had to promote the program content; but now we also had to sell the delivery concept. People understandably were not familiar with this new way of receiving information. They needed to feel comfortable about how it would work. We expect familiarity to increase by our next round of offerings because many people had a positive experience with the first telecast and have spread the word to others. Also, our potential audience is being barraged by journal and newspaper articles, TV and cable networks, and, in many instances, neighbors, that describe or have experienced satellite technology.

Even though dishes are cheaper and more accessible now and the audience is a bit more familiar with the delivery technology, we have not lessened our marketing efforts. We have broadened our market beyond the obvious audience (state rehabilitation counselors) to include all the rehabilitation professionals. The audience now includes private rehabilitation workers, special education, post-secondary handicapped student services personnel, social security disability examiners, social workers, employee assistance and workers within industry, the Veterans Administration, and professionals in speciality areas such as multiple sclerosis, cancer, and the aged.

Work Plan for Satellite Conferencing

The center has prepared a work plan for its next round of telecasts with two precepts in mind.

First, limited staff and financial resources dictate that the telecast content should be produced (in the can, if preproduced; scripted, if live) before any marketing effort, technology coordination, or network management activity begins. All major network components cannot be handled simultaneously without overburdening staff.

Second, the target audience is not homogeneous; audience members are not employees of one major organization. Our audience comes from many different organizations. Each requires development and this implies a variety of marketing approaches.

With these two major pointss in mind, we described in our plan only the network's major activities (see Fig. 8-2). The schedule is geared is geared to four or more telecasts. The activities are:

1. Logistics: Preparation of record keeping systems for the budget, billing and registrations, mailing lists, drafts of publication advertisements and brochures; phone staff briefed with information for potential attendees.

2. Marketing: Identification of major target organizations and personal contact with each organization's most influential member for gaining internal support and promotion. It is hoped that these individuals will "champion" the network to organization members. Identification and contracting with site facilitators.

3. Advertising: Identification of, and contracting with, appropriate periodicals for full page advertisements and final draft and sequential mailing of brochures. The first brochure provides general details applicable to all telecasts. Subsequent brochures promote a particular program three to four months in advance.

4. Satellite network: Reservation of uplink facility, receiving sites, and satellite time.

5. Content: All programs produced prior to initiation of any other major action.

6. Evaluation: Post-evaluation on the day of telecast (on-site) and three to six months later (remote). The on-site basically records approval/disapproval. The remote captures content implementation. Remote also keeps us in touch with target audience.

THE TIME TABLE

Month	1	2	3	4	5	6	7	8	9	10	16
Activity											
1. Content (done before)											
2. Logistics	1										
3. Marketing	1	2									
4. Advertise											
Brochure I			3								
Brochures				4	5	6	7				
5. Satellite		2									
6. Telecasts							7	8	9	10	
7. Evaluation											
On site							7	8	9	10	
Remote											16

Fig. 8-2 A special-event video teleconference requires the explicit application of project management tools such as this project time table.

CONCLUDING REFLECTIONS

It takes a lot of effort to produce a special event teleconference. One should plan to complete activities at different times and allow more than enough lead time for each.

For the type of training we were doing, we found preproduced training segments helped us to increase quality, improve control of time and material, decrease complexity of the production at the origination site, and thus save money. This does not mean that preproduction of video tapes is the only strategy. In fact, we are considering some programs which would not use preproduced tapes and whose training goals and styles would be quite different. We will lessen the emphasis on developing skills and increase the emphasis on simple information diffusion.

We learned that the uplink site does not need extensive production capacity if the training program is designed to use adequately the facilities available. We will probably continue to use only limited production features at the time of the telecast in order to reduce complexity and focus our attention on the content. In the future, we will carefully investigate the "redundancy" of the uplink and have contingency plans worked out for technical problems that may arise. We will probably buy insurance to protect ourselves against technical failures. (There are policies available for this.)

If we use rented downlink sites, we will specify more clearly our expectations for the training facility. We hope that we can work with the sites to improve their capacity. We are finding that many sites are quite interested in doing this as more become aware of the revenue potential of being a training site for teleconferences. We hope that interested organizations and associations will purchase their own dishes and create their own downlink facilities.

To any organization considering a satellite teleconference for the first time we would also recommend talking with experienced teleconferencers. We called and discussed this diffusion technique with any such person we could identify, and all were most willing to share helpful information.

THE AUTHORS

Mr. David A Molinaro is a Training Associate and Network Coordinator for the West Virginia Research and Training Center of West Virginia University. Mr. Molinaro has produced several multimedia learning packages and has published articles and conducted frequent workshops in telecommunications. He is currently a doctoral student in higher education teleconferencing at West Virginia University.

Mr. Dave Whipp is responsible for audio-visual production at the Research and Training Center. In addition to producing training materials in most media during his eight years at the center, he has also published articles and trained on subjects such as media use, telecommunications, and computers. Mr. Whipp holds degrees in English literature and education from West Virginia University.

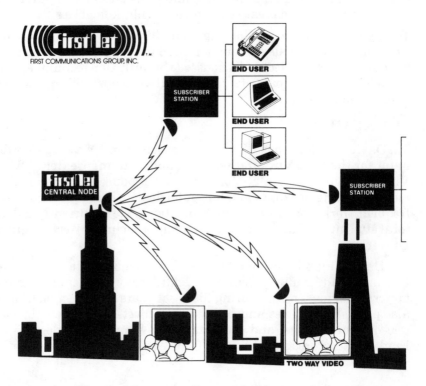

The future of the rapidly expanding market is reported, and suggestions for further investigation by the reader are offered.

Chapter 9
Conclusion: The Future for Video Teleconferencing
Ronald J. Bohm

THE MARKET FOR VIDEO TELECONFERENCING

According to Quantum Science, the New York research firm, the number of installed audiographic, stop-action, and continuous-motion video teleconferencing systems will grow from 575 in 1981 to 4,340 by 1986. They project the mix of systems will be 1,165 continuous-motion centers, 1,425 stop-action systems, and 1,750 audiographic systems. The market research firm expects audiographic systems to grow most rapidly in popularity until 1985 when it projects continuous-motion video teleconferencing will experience the fastest growth through 1991.

In current dollars, Quantum Science projects the market will grow to $520.3 million in 1986 from the 1981 level of only $19.3 million. Quantum Science bases these sales figures on a projected growth to 1.8 million business meetings using teleconference by 1986 from the 1981 level of 90,000. Considering the embryonic state of the video teleconferencing market, this 20-fold growth in five years is not astonishing. They attribute the bright prospects for the growth of teleconferencing to the emergence of AT&T as a market leader and the evolution of other "turn-key" system providers.

Looking into its crystal ball, Quantum foresees the use of desk-to-desk teleconferencing in which full-page touch sensitive monitors, facsimile, and computer files are used to share text and graphic information over the telephone network. Of course this evolution will require a continuation of the recent trends toward miniaturization and production quantity manufacturing. As if to confirm the prediction, in September 1983, Hewlett Packard announced it would produce the first personal computer to include a touch-sensitive monitor.

Creative Strategies takes a more conservative posture on the future size of the video teleconferencing equipment market. Projecting a 59% compound growth rate from 1983 to 1987, the San Jose research firm sees sales of equipment and services topping $430 million in 1987. Regardless of which forecast turns out to be more accurate, it seems clear that video teleconferencing is finally becoming established in the American business scene.

USER SATISFACTION
WITH VIDEO TELECONFERENCING

Both M/A-COM, Inc. and Aetna Life & Casualty (see Chapter 3) were cited in a Satellite Business Systems/Booz Allen & Hamilton survey which indicated that 9 of 10 users of video teleconferencing were either satisfied, or very satisfied, with their systems. The survey included all of the companies which had been using video teleconferencing for at least one year, for at least 20 hours per month. The other companies in the survey were Exxon, Hughes Aircraft, Deere & Company, General Telephone & Electronics, IBM, Mutual Insurance, Proctor & Gamble, and Sperry Corp.

The survey also found that:

- One-third experienced an improvement in the quality of decision making;

- Seventy five percent of the respondents reported an increase in personal productivity resulting from video teleconferencing;

- Fifty percent of those surveyed felt there was an increase in overall communication within the company, and many of these felt the result was greater responsiveness to a changing world;

- Fifty percent reported increased meeting effectiveness;

- Seventy-five percent reported reduced travel expenses; and

- Seventy-five percent reported a decrease in time spent away from the office.

Of all the respondents, only ten percent were dissatisfied with the results of their video teleconferencing experiences.

From the results of this study, it is clear that the savings in travel budgets could very well be one of the least important reasons to consider video teleconferencing. If improved decision making results in the aversion of one crisis or fiasco, the cost of video telecon-

ferencing could well be returned several fold. Several of the chapters in this book describe the intangible benefits derived from the use of video teleconferencing.

For those who feel more comfortable with tangible, objective comparisons, we offer some suggestions for analyzing the travel/teleconference tradeoff. In computing the cost of "meeting savings" of a teleconference, the following items should also be considered:

- Air travel expense;
- Employee salary while the employee is away, including travel time;
- Lodging expense;
- Meal expense;
- Tips, garaging, tolls, taxis;
- Long distance calls back to the home office while away as well as calls to the family;
- And, perhaps most important of all, the setbacks in all of the travelers' other projects and duties while away.

WHERE TO GET MORE INFORMATION

The University of Wisconsin-Extension at Madison

The University of Wisconsin-Extension at Madison provides a wealth of pamphlets, books, and directories of current activities in all aspects of teleconferencing through its Center for Interactive Programs. The Center offers frequent seminars, often using teleconferencing as the medium. Each spring, CIP sponsors an international conference on teleconferencing.

For additional information on CIP's programs and reference material, call (608) 262-4342.

The Telespan Newsletter

The *Telespan Newsletter* published by Elliot Gold in Altadena, California, offers profiles of teleconference implementations and current events. Gold also offers *The Definitive Guide to Teleconferencing Products and Services* which lists suppliers of systems, equipment, and services.

For additional information, call (213) 797-5482

The International Teleconferencing Association

The International Teleconferencing Association, was formed in 1982 to represent the teleconference user community. Additional information on ITCA is available by calling (703) 556-6115.

The Teleconferencing Association of Canada

Also recently formed was the Teleconferencing Association of Canada, based in Toronto. Information may be obtained by calling (416) 231-8665.